T0114000

Praise for *Love Never Dies*

"Dr. Turndorf has written a remarkably moving chronicle of her own life, and uses it as a spiritually insightful guide to effectively help others. The art form for spirit communication, described in this book, will not only make it possible for you to connect with departed loved ones, but also bring true harmony into your everyday life."

— **Dannion Brinkley**, New York Times best-selling
author of *Saved by the Light*

*"Dr. Turndorf shows us the way to heal our hearts
and find lasting love."*

— **John Gray**, Ph.D., #1 *New York Times* best-selling author of *Men Are
from Mars, Women Are from Venus*

"Dr. Turndorf's eternal love story powerfully proves that our loved ones in spirit are waiting for us to reconnect with them! Read this amazing book and discover her groundbreaking new dialoguing technique, which enables you to reconnect and turn grief into peace and joy."

— **Mira Kelley**, best-selling author of *Beyond Past Lives*

"Dr. Turndorf's extraordinary memoir/self-help book provides astonishing proof that we don't die and that we are meant to reconnect and stay connected to loved ones in spirit. Read this book, learn her powerful new method for reconnecting and making peace with the deceased, and you will transform your grief to joy."

— **Fr. Richard Rohr**, founder of the Center for Action and
Contemplation (CAC) and best-selling author of *Falling Upward*

"I found the book very helpful in guiding people to learn how to tune in to spirit messages, and particularly liked Dr. Turndorf's guidance through meditations. In Parts II and III, Dr. Turndorf covered so many of the ways that spirits convey messages, and this book will be a great help for people trying to get in touch with their loved ones.
"Part I was her story of losing the love of her life. Reading about the pain and agony she experienced—and so many people experience—will be healing to others experiencing the same emotions after the passing of a loved one. I think the first part could be a book on its own merit because it is so beneficial to people dealing with the same intensity of grief.
"As a scientist myself, I was glad to read that Dr. Turndorf didn't focus on a religion. As a medium, I have come to know that 'god' is not of a

religion, but is the consciousness of all living things. Like Dr. Turndorf, I've learned that all people are equal, and all creatures are part of all existence (and have 'souls').
"I particularly enjoyed reading how she used her mediumship talent to help people overcome their grief. Readers will get a lot out of this book and know that their loved ones are always connected."

— **Rob Gutro**, author, medium, and scientist

"I could not put this book down! It is so gripping from the first few words, and beautifully written. Dr. Turndorf's courageous story of her reunion with her beloved husband after his death and the heartfelt stories of others serve to validate what many may have privately experi-enced but discounted as just a by-product of grief and loss and not really 'real.' The book's simple and powerful techniques provide essential tools for connecting to loved ones in spirit and will allow scientists to amass new data from laypeople, apart from mediums. Dr. Turndorf's book will make a profound contribution to the now significant scientific data al-ready collected in laboratories around the world studying survival of in-dividual consciousness after death, while adding richly to our own sense of love and peace. I am thankful for her gift!"

— **Linda G. Russek, Ph.D.**, former co-founder and co-director of the Human Energy Systems Laboratory, University of Arizona, and co-author of *The Living Energy Universe*

"This is the most beautiful true love story that I have ever read. The depth of the author's love for her husband, her terrible grief at his death, and then her triumph as she learned to continue her relation-ship with him even after his death are all palpable. I lived it with her, and her story has stayed in my mind. For me, though, the reason to read this book is the author's wisdom in teaching her readers how to heal rifts across the death boundary. As one who has done extensive afterlife research, I can attest to the importance of post-death healing of relationships to both our dead loved ones and ourselves! Yet few people know how essential this healing is, and fewer still know how to begin it. As a prominent relationship counselor, Dr. Turndorf tackles this essential area, and she does it well. Hers is a wonderful book."

— **Roberta Grimes**, best-selling author of *The Fun of Dying* and *The Fun of Staying in Touch*

love

NEVER DIES

ALSO BY DR. JAMIE TURNDORF

*KISS YOUR FIGHTS GOOD-BYE: Dr. Love's 10 Simple Steps to Cooling Conflict and Rekindling Your Relationship**

DR. LOVE'S COUPLES' GUIDE TO SURVIVING THE JOLLY HOLLERDAYS

MAKE UP DON'T BREAK UP: Dr. Love's 5-Step Plan for Reconciling with Your Ex

THE PLEASURE OF YOUR COMPANY: A Socio-Psychological Analysis of Modern Sociability (with Emile Jean Pin)

*Available from Hay House

Please visit:

Hay House USA: www.hayhouse.com®
Hay House Australia: www.hayhouse.com.au
Hay House UK: www.hayhouse.co.uk
Hay House India: www.hayhouse.co.in

love

NEVER DIES

HOW TO **RECONNECT** AND
MAKE PEACE WITH THE DECEASED

DR. JAMIE TURNDORF

HAY HOUSE, INC.
Carlsbad, California • New York City
London • Sydney • New Delhi

Copyright © 2014 by Jamie Turndorf

Published in the United States by: Hay House, Inc.: www.hayhouse.com® • **Published in Australia by:** Hay House Australia Pty. Ltd.: www.hayhouse.com.au • **Published in the United Kingdom by:** Hay House UK, Ltd.: www.hayhouse.co.uk • **Published in India by:** Hay House Publishers India: www.hayhouse.co.in

Cover design: Angela Moody • *Interior design:* Riann Bender

Library of Congress Cataloging-in-Publication Data

Turndorf, Jamie.
  Love never dies : how to reconnect and make peace with the deceased / Jamie Turndorf.
      pages cm
   ISBN 978-1-4019-4534-3 (hardback)
  1. Grief therapy. 2. Death. 3. Mind and body. 4. Spirituality. I. Title.
  RC455.4.L67T87 2014
  155.9'37--dc23
                                        2014016306

Tradepaper ISBN: 978-1-4019-4535-0

1st edition, August 2014
2nd edition, August 2015

Printed in the United States of America

Lost and Found
On the day you were lowered into the ground
Our love for each other wasn't lost but found

To my beloved Jean Pin:
Soon after you left your body, I learned that the Dalai Lama
publicly prayed for you, honoring you as one of the 50 people of all
time who was one with God. Since God is love, it was no wonder
that you devoted your life on Earth to loving me ever more perfectly.
Your ongoing devotion to our relationship remains the greatest and
most astonishing gift of my life. This book is my answer to your
request that I share our story with the world, so that "our love may
shine like a torch that lights the path for others."

CONTENTS

PREFACE

As a young girl I received a detailed premonition of the man I would someday marry. For this reason, although I always enjoyed male company, I saw no point in seriously dating anyone. I was content to wait until that man eventually entered my life.

And he did appear, on the first day of my freshman year at Vassar College in Poughkeepsie, New York. Oddly, when I was a young child, whenever we took a family road trip, I'd ask my father, "Where are we?" To which he would jokingly respond, "Poughkeepsie." In retrospect, I realize that destiny was leading me to this town where I would find my Jean many years later.

On the first day of my freshman year, I creaked open the heavy oak door of Blodgett Hall and bounded up the steps, two at a time, to the third floor, where the offices of the sociology department were located. Having been shut out of all the sections of the Introduction to Sociology course, I was determined to finagle a place for myself in one of the closed classes. The secretary told me that only the department chair, a professor named Jean Pin, had the authority to make an exception.

The moment I stepped into Jean's office, I felt my soul leave my body. I felt as though I were being transported at high speed through a tunnel to what I knew was the end of my life. I saw a white light at the end of the tunnel, but, unlike a near-death experience, I didn't meet deceased loved ones. I just went on a journey that was out of time and place, lasting seconds and lasting a lifetime. When I was jolted back into my body, I received a message that told me, *Remember every aspect of your meeting . . . He will be everything to you one day.*

Oddly, this amazing premonition didn't shock me, despite my not knowing where it came from or why. I soon forgot about it, the way a patient unconsciously represses a therapeutic breakthrough that occurs before it is time to integrate the information. In my case, it was too soon for me to act upon this knowledge, whatever its source, so my mind just let it go. I attended the Intro to Sociology class that first semester and continued my life as a college student.

I LATER LEARNED THAT PRIOR TO COMING to Vassar, Jean had been one of the most famous Jesuit priests in history. A Renaissance man to the core, he held a doctor of letters from the Sorbonne; a doctorate in sociology; and higher degrees in classics, religion, law and economics, political science, history, and philosophy.

His first book, *Pratique Religieuse et Classes Sociales Dans une Paroisse Urbaine (Religious Practices and Social Classes in an Urban Parish)*, captured the attention and admiration of Pope Paul VI, who subsequently called Jean to Rome to teach.

Apart from his teaching at the Vatican, Jean founded CIRIS, the Vatican's first and only international social-research center. He taught himself ten languages and then traveled the world conducting face-to-face interviews to determine if the church was meeting the needs of the faithful. His methods became the standard for all sociological research that followed. He published books and articles in many languages and changed the way the church ministered to the faithful.

Jean was also one of the founding fathers of the liberation theology movement, which was established to fight church oppression from within. His struggle for religious freedom gained him international fame when he publicly denounced the Catholic Church and Pope Paul VI for their attempts to block the legalization of divorce in Italy. His efforts ultimately proved successful and helped change the course of Italian history.

As a celebrity priest, he rubbed elbows during the day with aristocrats, kings, movie stars (Audrey Hepburn was his good friend), and the intelligentsia of Rome and the rest of Europe. Then each night he would return to his monastery to sleep!

At the time of our first meeting, Jean was married to a German. Their union occurred after the pope granted him the dispensation of his vows, when he was laicized and left the priesthood. Even though he was laicized, which meant that he wasn't excommunicated, he knew that famous ex-priests were shunned in Europe. He told me later that he was recognized even without his clerical garb. Because he knew it would be impossible for him to find work in Europe, he came to America, where he was recruited by Vassar College to serve as a full professor and chair of the department of sociology

While the pope had freed Jean from his vows to the Jesuit order and the church, he soon found himself chained to a loveless long-distance marriage. His wife lived in New York City and he in Poughkeepsie.

On the day I met him, Jean had been married for ten years and was utterly miserable.

ONE DAY, WITHOUT HIS REALIZING that he was being observed, I saw Jean walking across the commons, his shoulders slumped in an attitude of defeat. Bound by the commitment he had made, he was serving out a life sentence, waiting to be paroled by death.

Three years after our fated meeting on that first day of my freshman year, I asked Professor Pin if he would help me analyze my data for my senior thesis. I had heard that, among other things, he was a statistician. Since my own advisor didn't know statistics, he was the perfect person to assist me. I'd taken two courses with him already and admired his intellect. Since I'd created an independent major within the department of American culture, which combined psychology and sociology and many other liberal-arts disciplines, a sociology professor was as logical a choice as any. Of course, beyond all these rational explanations, it was the pull of the tide of fate that drew me inexorably to him.

We met in his tiny college apartment. To the sound of clicking calculator buttons, we computed my data while talking our hearts out. Despite our different cultural backgrounds, generations (he was 58 and I was 21), and religions, our love ignited like a flash fire.

Despite our shared passion, which grew as time went by, and even though he had never consummated his marriage, Jean told me that he had made a lifetime vow to his wife. He said that he would have to end our relationship if she found out about us.

A YEAR LATER, SHE DID FIND OUT. I was driving north on the Taconic State Parkway, heading for Jean's apartment, when I saw a gray VW Beetle racing south. I refused to believe that it was *his* VW that had just whizzed past.

When I reached his apartment, I realized that it *had* been his car and that he had left me. He'd propped a note on his desk. It stood at attention like an obedient soldier carrying out his orders. He wrote that his wife had discovered our affair and that he was headed for New York City.

I drove to my college friend James's house in New Hampshire. A couple of days later, Jean tracked me down and phoned to tell me that he was sorry—it was over. He said he'd had a wonderful time with me. I heard him crying into the phone. He was hissing and gasping for breath.

I shrieked into the phone, emitting the agonized yelp of a wounded animal. He had torn my heart from my chest.

I slammed the phone down.

James took me out to his lake cabin. He rowed me to the center of the lake, where my wrenching sobs reverberated against the trees in the lonely forest surrounding us.

THAT SUMMER JEAN TRAVELED TO TURKEY with his wife, where—he told me later—he wept each day. He couldn't eat and had lost a great deal of weight. People thought he was dying of cancer.

At the end of his summer trip, he delivered a lecture at a sociology conference in Italy. At the conference, he met a young female sociologist. One day, he broke down and told her our story. He concluded the story by proudly reporting what he thought was his ultimate act of self-sacrifice—returning to his wife.

The young woman snapped at him, *"Stronzone*—idiot. The woman you left was your true wife. You waited your entire life to find this woman and discover love. She was the one who gave you your manhood. She is your true wife!"

That young scholar was surely an angel, for it was her confrontation that catapulted Jean into emotional upheaval. He realized that his sense of duty was misguided. He was not doing his wife or himself any service (quite literally!) by making such an unbearable sacrifice.

He left his wife and was divorced soon afterward. On September 17 (the exact month and day that his father had died years earlier, and the exact month and day that he himself would die 25 years later), 1981, Jean wrote me a note and a poem that he composed, saying that he was separated and soon to be divorced. He was now free to be with me, if I would have him.

FOR NEARLY 30 YEARS OUR LOVE burned brighter with each day.

We were beyond compatible, beyond twin flames. We were soul mates, the ultimate in physical and spiritual compatibility. We loved the same activities, music, and hobbies. We wrote books together, ran businesses together, restored and decorated houses together, and rejoiced in every moment that we spent together. We were, in a word, inseparable.

Jean had clearly been waiting to find me, as much as I had waited for him to finally appear. He always promised to live to be very old so we could die together. Thankfully, he was a very healthy man. But in the last year of his life, we both began having premonitions about his imminent death. We both had seen that he was going to die from an accident—that much we knew—but we didn't know when or where.

One night in 2006, I lay in bed with my head on his shoulder. Out of nowhere he said, "Jamie, I won't be able to keep my word and live to be very old and die with you."

"I know," I responded. "You're going to die of an accident."

He said that he knew this, too.

I said, "Then I will be alone for the rest of my life."

To which he responded, "You won't be alone. I'm going to send you my clone."

"There is no clone of you," I replied adamantly. "There can only be one Jean Pin."

I'll never forget the enigmatic smile on his face when he said, "You will see, Jamie. You will see."

That's where the conversation ended. But, as I was about to discover, I *would* soon see!

SOON AFTERWARD, WE DEPARTED for a vacation in Europe, despite the growing sense of foreboding I had about the upcoming trip. Before we left, I saw a large multitude of black crows in our garden. I tried to shrug off my concerns but was unable to shake the feeling of impending doom.

Despite these warnings, we journeyed to Sperlonga, Italy, where we'd enjoyed vacations before. Perched high upon rocky cliffs, the whitewashed fortified walls of this ancient Roman resort town towered majestically above the endless blue blanket of the bay below. Whitecaps fluttered like strips of lace bobbing up and down in the unusually choppy water.

It rained for days, as if the sky was weeping in anticipation of what was to come. A few days into the trip, Jean told me that he loved me so much that he would gladly take a bullet for me. My stomach knotted. His words chimed like yet another omen in the wind.

When the sky finally cleared, we headed to the beach. As we were talking, I noticed that Jean had raised his left hand above his head, as if to block the rays of the sun. Suddenly, a bee swooped down and stung his left hand, just below his index finger (at the exact location, I would learn, of Christ's stigmata wound). As soon as he was stung, I thought, *He's been struck by a bolt of lightning. He's dead.*

Jean told me the sting was excruciatingly painful, and that the venom went very deep.

I kissed the palm of my beloved husband and told him that it would feel better soon. I cupped my hand, gathered some seawater, and sprinkled it on his palm.

EARLY THE NEXT MORNING, after Jean told me he was having trouble breathing, we drove immediately to the local hospital.

There, I watched a doctor inject him with what we were told was cortisone. Months later, I discovered that it was actually an asthma drug—a gross error. Nevertheless, the discharge summary confirmed no heart attack and normal blood pressure.

We returned to the hotel elated over Jean's clean bill of health, again rejoicing that he didn't suffer the problems that often afflict older people. Before we left on vacation, Jean's doctor had told him that he had the body of a young man, despite his 84 years. He had low blood pressure, low cholesterol, and boundless energy. I used to tease him by saying that I was too old for him, and that he needed to find a younger wife. In fact, this was no joke. I had a hard time keeping up with him.

That night it was cold and rainy as we drove to La Nave restaurant. We dined indoors, holding hands, our hearts and minds focused on each other and not the dismal weather outside.

After the meal we drove back to the hotel, where Jean kissed me with such passion that I felt as though my heart were about to rupture, unable to contain the love I felt for him. Miraculously, our passion hadn't waned despite the passage of decades.

THE NEXT DAY, SPLINTERS OF RAIN gave way to hints of sun. I walked to the beach and napped under a steel-wool sky. When Jean found me there, my heart swelled and then melted with joy—as if I were being reunited with my loved one after too long an absence.

Clouds converged and when it started raining again, we ducked under the overhang near the pool. Serenaded by the patter of raindrops and a whisper of wind, we kissed as young lovers do.

Later that afternoon, Jean confessed to me that despite the injection the hospital had given him, he could still feel the venom coursing through his veins.

I opened the balcony door and invited him to lie down on the bed for a massage. The sea breeze and my own hands combined efforts to caress his skin and ease the tension out of him. When I finished my ministrations, he gave me an angelic smile.

I asked him why.

He said, "I feel how much you love me."

As we dressed for dinner, I admired my handsome husband as he adjusted his silk tie. How was it possible that after so many years of marriage, my heart still skittered and my loins still stirred whenever I looked at him? Silver hair framing a nearly lineless aristocratic face, impish eyes that sparkled with humor, a smile that made my heart skip a beat, an adorable slender body that was always impeccably dressed . . . so distinguished, cultured and elegant, gentle and kind. When it came to how much I loved this man, I soon ran out of adjectives.

We kissed and walked arm in arm, like newlyweds. Talking about everything and nothing, we folded ourselves into our tiny Fiat rental car.

I was driving and he pointed me in the direction of Punta Rossa, an elegant restaurant perched atop rouge-colored cliffs. After driving for 45 minutes, however, we were clearly lost.

I parked in front of a pizza dive and Jean went inside to get directions. After about ten minutes, he came out looking as white as a sheet, terror clearly written upon his face.

I asked what was wrong.

"We have to get back to the hospital," he managed. "I can't breathe."

I could hear him struggling for air. Fluid was rattling in his lungs, rising like a deluge that threatened to drown him.

I sped along the road mumbling something, anything that might reassure him. That might reassure *me*.

"You have what babies get," I babbled. "It's like the croup. Don't worry. The hospital will help you." I looked askance at him. "I love you," I said, with all the conviction my heart could hold.

"I love you," he told me.

These were the last words he ever spoke to me. He didn't have enough air in his lungs to utter another word.

As I sped along, I held tightly to his left wrist, hoping against hope that my hand would anchor him to the earth.

After about 20 minutes, I screeched into the hospital parking lot and ran inside.

I found a cluster of people in the waiting room, but no one at the admitting desk.

I recognized one of the two men who had treated Jean the day before. I don't speak Italian, but God help me, I found the words: *"Mi marito non posso respirare. Puntura d'ape ieri."* My husband can't breathe. Bee sting yesterday.

A paramedic followed me outside pushing a wheelchair, plodding forward like an overfed buffalo in a heat wave. With some difficulty he settled Jean into the chair and wheeled him into the treatment room, where an oxygen mask was placed on his face. But the paramedic had trouble finding Jean's vein because his blood vessels were constricted from the venom. Finally, a needle was inserted and the IV began to drip. I was assured that my husband would feel better once the bottle was fully infused.

Jean was ripping at the oxygen mask, obviously feeling that it was suffocating him because the air wasn't getting into his lungs. He was covered in sweat, and his hair was plastered to his scalp.

I could hear the fluid in his lungs, filling them with its vile poison. I was dying watching him suffer in agony.

I asked the hospital staff to tilt up the head of the bed. They did. After a few minutes, when there was no improvement, I asked if they had a *polmone specialista*, a pulmonologist.

They didn't answer me, which meant no.

Even to my untrained eye, it was obvious that Jean needed a tracheotomy. The doctor treating him was an anesthesiologist, and she didn't seem to know much about this procedure. She kept beating her hand in the air like an angry librarian scolding a noisy child, admonishing him to breathe slowly and deeply, perhaps assuming he was hyperventilating from panic.

It was painfully clear that Jean couldn't breathe—slowly or otherwise. Didn't they hear that his lungs were full of fluid? He was drowning. He had no air *to* breathe.

I removed his watch, trying everything in my power to make my beloved boy more comfortable.

They brought over a garbage pail and dropped it on the floor in front of him. I held him from behind as he gagged to expel the thick mucus that had risen to the back of his throat.

The IV bottle was empty now. I asked if he felt better. He shook his head no.

When I shouted at the staff to do something, they produced a syringe.

"*Adrenalina,*" they said. As they prepared an enormous needle to insert into his neck, they pushed me out into the waiting room. My last sight of Jean alive was his eyes rolling up in their sockets as he slipped into unconsciousness.

I never got to kiss him or tell him good-bye.

In the waiting room I was hysterical, shaking, panting, begging, using broken Italian and hand gestures to try to get someone to help me summon an air ambulance from Rome.

I asked the name of the *numero uno hospedale a Roma,* the number one hospital in Rome. I was told Gemelli. But the only way to get Jean transferred there would be for this hospital to call Gemelli. The people in the waiting room told me not to bother asking, because the hospital would not spend the money to make the call. They added, as if explaining the reason why, that this hospital was not a very good hospital.

I banged on the door and begged them to call anyway. They dismissed me and advised me to be patient.

I said, "He's going to die. He has no air."

They pushed me away and locked the door behind me.

I tried to use the pay phone to call Rome myself, but it was broken. I banged on the door again and asked if I could use the phone in the inner office. They told me no.

I could hear Jean's tortured attempts to breathe through the door. I couldn't believe how long he held on with no air. How strong his heart was, how desperately he fought to live for me.

A little later someone came out once and told me, "We're trying to get the fluid out of his lungs." Another time, a doctor came out to ask me if Jean was taking any medications. He wasn't. There wasn't a thing wrong with him.

After what seemed an eternity, a man came into the waiting room wearing a defeated expression on his face. He told me in Italian that they were sorry; they had done everything they could.

I collapsed in a woman's arms. The crowd barraged me with questions. Was I alone in Italy? Did I have any children? Where was I staying?

Someone from the medical staff came out again. In a daze I told him that I wanted Jean's rings and clothing.

In reply, he said that Italian law requires that I be present when they remove them from his body.

He said, "Come. It's fine."

I tentatively followed behind him like a child afraid of her first dental visit. He led me down a corridor, and we entered the room where Jean was laid out on a gurney. His face was as red as a lobster and his mouth was wide open. His body was as stiff as a board.

I ran out screaming. They tried to give me something to drink that would pacify me. I wouldn't swallow it, afraid in my near delirium that they were going to kill me, too.

I left our rental car in the parking lot and Bruno, an employee at the hotel, drove me back to my room. I was sure that I would never be able to scrub the image of Jean's body from my mind. Never would I stop hearing the rattling sound of him suffocating to death.

I vaguely recall holding Jean's clothing, minus his pants, and thinking, *In death a person soils himself.* I felt embarrassed on his behalf, outraged that such an elegant man should have been forced to suffer such an indignity.

BACK IN THE HOTEL ROOM, I FELL ONTO the bed. The sound of his suffocating droned in my head like an endless stutter. Etched into my brain was the image of my sweet love's beautiful face turned scarlet. The pain in my heart seared my chest. My ears felt as if they would rupture from the sound of my pounding heart. I was sure I was dying of a heart attack—or of a heart broken.

I collapsed onto my side of the bed, crying and trembling in terror. I felt as though I'd free-fallen into an abyss of grief and despair.

Suddenly I felt a gentle caress that extended the length of my spine.

I glanced over my shoulder. Nothing. No one was there.

This was the first of Jean's visitations. He has been with me ever since.

INTRODUCTION

Many of my colleagues have urged me not to write this book, fearing that I will lose my reputation as a respected professional. During earlier times in history, I might well have been imprisoned or burned at the stake for daring to tell this story. While I no longer risk internment or interment, sharing this story is tantamount to pinning a giant bull's-eye on my chest. For those who strike out in fear, my story will be seen as an engraved invitation to attack the messenger who rattles the cage of conformity.

I am aware that some closed-minded individuals will declare me a delusional madwoman and write me off as a nut—not the best diagnosis for a shrink! As it happens, I'm a fairly famous shrink, a woman of science who holds a doctorate in psychology.

Known worldwide as Dr. Love, I have authored the critically acclaimed book *Kiss Your Fights Good-bye: Dr. Love's 10 Simple Steps to Cooling Conflict and Rekindling Your Relationship.* I'm also the creator of the award-winning website askdrlove.com (the web's first relationship-advice site), which has drawn up to three million hits per month; the host of the popular *Ask Dr. Love* radio show; a frequent guest on television and radio; and a contributor to national and international websites, newspapers, and magazines.

As founder/director of the Center for Emotional Communication, I have spent the past 31 years perfecting my Core Therapy method. This cutting-edge healing process enables people to unearth and mend what I call Old Scars, which interfere with our ability to establish and maintain loving relationships with others and with ourselves.

As long as we're talking about me, you should know that it's not at all comfortable for me to speak about my personal life. As a shrink I've been trained to be a "blank screen," to not disclose myself, especially to my patients. However, to honor my husband's postmortem request that I tell our story, I am forcing myself to not hold back, to share even the most intimate details with you. Believe me, a daily root canal would be an easier regimen to follow!

While the story I share is factual, I have changed the names of most of my patients (except those who expressly said that they did not mind having their names used) to protect their privacy. All the other names presented in this book are true.

God and Spirit

As you read Jean's and my story, you will notice that I refer to God at various points. I use the term generically. Perhaps you are spiritual and don't practice any formal religion. Or perhaps you worship Allah, Yahweh, Krishna, Shangdi, Bhagavan, the Goddess, the Creator, or a Higher Power. No matter—as Jean told me soon after his death, "We're all one family. We're all one religion. That religion is love."

Speaking of God, while Jean's life was steeped in religion, I was raised by two Jewish atheists. The only religion my parents practiced was religiously hating each other! While still wearing diapers, I swear I had earned an unofficial Ph.D. degree in psychology from mediating my parents' fights. It is said that shrinks enter the profession as a result of growing up in utterly dysfunctional families. In my case, what actually drove me to select my career was having spent the first three months of my life alone in the preemie nursery. According to a psychic I know, this painful isolation gave birth to my ministry of connecting souls—I didn't want others to suffer the agony of isolation that I'd experienced. As for my family, I never went to synagogue with them or read the Bible. In fact, my parents taught me to *not* believe in God or the afterlife.

My lack of belief was abruptly shattered after Jean's death. His miraculous manifestations, often in front of witnesses, prove that there is life after life. From the beginning of time, humans have hoped and prayed that an afterlife exists. Traditionally, the belief has been based on a leap of faith rather than a confirmed reality.

Overcoming the Two Universal Fears

Jean has asked me to tell our story in order to ease the two most universal and dreaded fears: that of loving and losing, and that of death and dying. The story I share is positive proof that relationships do not cease with death and that what Paul said in his first letter to the Corinthians is true: Love never ends.

It is important to note that the other books that discuss spirit contact generally offer compilations of stories from many different individuals, each of whom describes a *single* spirit visitation from one being. By contrast, this book presents *multiple* manifestations from *one* spirit being, as well as manifestations my clients have experienced with their own loved (and hated) ones in spirit form.

While it is easy to dismiss single visitations as flukes or figments of the observers' imaginations, the sheer magnitude of the manifestations from one spirit being provides unequivocal proof of the existence of an afterlife.

As another point of difference, the single visits that are presented in other books correspond to the way Westerners approach grief—grieve, let go, and move on. I contend that these single contacts are the result of religious indoctrination. Since Jean left his body, I have learned that Christians are taught that once in heaven, a spirit being is permanently out of reach and therefore unable to engage in ongoing—or any—contact with the living. Because our experiences are governed by expectations, the belief that ongoing contact is impossible is sufficient to prevent people from being open to the signs demonstrating that our loved ones in spirit are continually reaching out to us.

Reactions to Our Story

Since 2006, I have been sharing our story with therapy clients and radio/web and lecture audiences. The reactions to our story are grouped into four distinct camps:

The first camp consists of people who are frightened by the prospect of connecting with the spirit realm. On the extreme end of that spectrum are those who are afraid that opening the ethereal door will allow evil spirits or even Satan himself to enter in. For these people, I offer the analogy of call blocking on a telephone. I explain that we, as intelligent human beings, have the ability to set boundaries for ourselves. Just as we can screen our incoming calls and refuse access to unwanted callers, the same can be done with unwanted spirit presences.

Your heart has the ability to discern the difference between love and evil, and you can simply refuse incoming messages that you don't wish to receive. I can't deny that evil spirits may exist; I just know that I have never had to deal with them. Jean acts as my gatekeeper. His love guards me against any negative presences (if there are any). Your loved ones in spirit are equally devoted to protecting you. Love *always* triumphs over evil.

The second group is immensely relieved and comforted to discover the truth. For these people, simply knowing that continued contact is possible allows them to begin their own process of healing and reconnecting with their loved ones.

The third group experiences a sense of jealousy, despair, hurt, or anger. These people invariably ask, "Why is your husband in contact with you? My loved one never comes to me!"

In response to this third group, I describe the various signs of spirit presence. In a matter of minutes, I'm hearing, "That happened to me . . . and so did that!" For members of this group, becoming aware of the signs is all that is needed to unlock the dead bolt of ignorance that has barred the door of their hearts. In no time, they, too, are peeking through, beholding their loved ones once more.

A fourth group comprises those who don't believe in an after-life. That's fine. I once belonged to this group myself. But even if you don't believe, you can still be healed using my dialoguing process.

There are also those who are afraid to admit that they've had spirit contact. This group is apt to hide in the shadows, fearing that others will think them odd or even insane. The telling of our story is liberating for these people: If a well-known shrink is will-ing to risk being labeled as crazy, then what do they have to lose by admitting their own experiences with spirit contact? It is my most devout hope that the telling of *our* story will enable people worldwide to begin telling their own stories, thereby inviting oth-ers to come out of the shadows.

Some people have voiced the objection that reconnecting with those who have passed over before us prevents us from "moving on" with our lives. The answer to this is simple: Our hearts are made to love. There is no limit to the number of people we can love, and more than enough room in our hearts to care for those who have passed over as well as those who walk the earth!

Another common misconception is the idea that our remain-ing in connection prevents our loved ones from "moving on." The concept of moving on is itself a misconception because our loved ones in spirit don't "go" anywhere. What's more, it has been prov-en to me again and again that our loved ones in spirit are devoted to standing by us and supporting us in life.

Beyond Traditional Western Grief Therapy

As a psychotherapist, I am aware that the traditional Western approach to grief (grieve, let go, and move on) often leaves the bereaved at an even greater loss. In fact, when writing this book I discovered that the Western psychiatric community has actually created new diagnostic labels for what they consider abnormal grief reactions. The result: The labels "Prolonged Grief Disorder" and "Complicated Grief Disorder" may be slapped on anyone who hasn't "snapped out of it" after six months.

If that's not bad enough, I was utterly shocked to discover that the psychiatric community considers hallucinations to be an integral part of these abnormal grief syndromes.

An article published in 1995 in the *American Journal of Psychiatry* states, "Preoccupation with thoughts of the deceased . . . disbelief regarding the death . . . and lack of acceptance of the death" are symptoms of these disorders. In other words, if you're open enough to admit that the spirit of your loved one lives on, and, God forbid, if you admit to seeing or hearing a deceased loved one in *any* form, psychiatrists can immediately assign a crippling label and tell you that you're hallucinating. This is not only ridiculous; it is appalling.

In an article published in 2005 by the *Journal of the American Medical Association* entitled "Treatment of Complicated Grief: A Randomized Controlled Trial," the authors state: "Estimates suggest each death leaves an average of 5 people bereaved, suggesting that more than 1 million people per year are expected to develop complicated grief in the United States."

What the establishment views as a pathological reaction to the loss of a loved one, or "complicated grief," I view as a higher state of consciousness! In other words, one million people are spiritually open enough to continue a relationship with someone who has passed without obtaining assistance in doing so. I can only hope to help countless more millions achieve this state.

The Birth of My New Trans-dimensional Grief-Therapy Method

As Jean's and my story unfolds, you'll notice my gradual discovery of my own mediumistic abilities. My realization that I could hear not only Jean but also other spirit beings motivated me to develop a groundbreaking grief-therapy method that guides the bereaved to reconnect rather than to say good-bye. Since 2006, I have been assisting grieving patients worldwide in doing just this, and the healing that has resulted is astonishing.

We can be in touch to whatever degree we desire. Reconnecting is especially vital for those who have lost a loved one to sudden illness or tragic death. These people have been robbed of the chance to say farewell and, if needed, to make amends.

While some may simply wish to reestablish contact in the early stages of loss to help work through the grieving process, there are many other cases in which ongoing connection is desirable. For example, reconnecting and staying connected is a lifeline, especially for the elderly who may not wish to form another primary attachment. Likewise, many parents who have lost children desperately need long-term contact, as do children who have lost parents.

My point is, reconnecting with a deceased loved one and staying connected is a form of healing that cannot be measured or prescribed. Of course, the wonder of it all is that, as you will see, you don't have to say *au revoir* to anyone dearly departed, because you can reunite with your loved ones sooner than you thought.

But reconnecting is just the beginning. Millions of people harbor resentment toward the deceased, often as a result of having been abused or mistreated by a parent, sibling, partner, or spouse who has since died. Unfortunately, traditional Western therapy offers no method for resolving this unfinished business. In contrast, my method provides a solution for the millions who suffer.

Inspired by Jean's revelations regarding the transformations that occur after death, I now know that when someone enters spirit form, that being has—at the very least—a clearer perspective on the mistakes that he or she made on Earth. This awareness sets the stage for reconciliation. While it's true that some beings are waiting with open arms to make peace and shower us with love, others may need a little more nudging. But even the most unevolved beings know that their own spiritual progression requires them to right their wrongs by making amends with those living here. This means that it's never too late to heal wounds, resolve resentments, make peace, and repair a damaged relationship with someone who has passed over; and that in death it is possible to resolve issues that never could have been addressed during a person's lifetime. (As one of my patients quipped, "I wish my mother would hurry up and die so we can work this out.")

About This Book

This book is divided into three parts. In the first part, you'll read about my ongoing experiences with Jean in spirit form following the night he left his body. I have attempted to present my experiences in chronological order so that you can share in my own burgeoning recognition of Jean's continued presence in my life. Keep in mind that my experiences with Jean were (and are) anything but linear. Simultaneously, he offered me a multitude of signs to let me know that he was (and is) right beside me. In addition to the signs, he also made his presence known by sending me messages through animals, who are what I call natural Open Vessels, and specific people who are also particularly open.

At the same time, Jean guided me to engage in dialogues with him through writing and oral conversations. I also learned to dialogue with him using what I call Earthly Props, in the form of electronic devices as well as animals and humans who are open. Using these props, we were able to engage in two-sided dialogues. As you'll see, it was through Jean's various signs and manifestations and our dialogues that he helped us to achieve a resolution to an outstanding issue that we struggled with, as well as guided me to heal myself mind, body, and soul, culminating in my realizing true self-love for the first time in my life.

As you read my experiences in Part I, I remind you that everything I share is the honest truth, word for word, detail for detail. I know what I report may be difficult for some readers to believe. I know the events are oftentimes quite shocking. I understand that abandoning familiar beliefs is scary, not unlike being lost in a foreign land where no one speaks your language. Because humans are creatures of habit, we prefer to cling to what we've been taught to believe and reject whatever doesn't correspond to our mind-sets. So as you read on, all I ask is that you temporarily adopt the innocence of a child; open your heart and mind; and suspend all preconceived notions about time, space, matter, this life, and the beyond.

The chapters in Part II are designed to help you dispel any beliefs that may hinder your own reconnection with spirit. In this section, I share Jean's messages revealing why what we've been told about the afterlife is "dead" wrong, if you'll pardon the pun, and why ongoing communication with spirit beings is not only possible but also desirable.

In Part III, I teach you how to reconnect with beings in spirit. In addition to connecting, you'll learn how to make peace, if needed, using my new method, which can best be described as spiritual relationship therapy. While an evidence medium offers vivid details that verify a spirit's presence and acts as an intermediary between those who have crossed over and those on Earth in a one-sided transmission, my method, by contrast, guides you to make your own direct contact *and* engage in a two-sided discussion.

As you will discover, you don't need a channeler, medium, or psychic to reconnect. In the final section of the book, you'll learn my three-part method:

1. Create a state of receptivity.

2. Recognize the signs of spirit presence.

3. Dialogue with the departed.

At the end of the book, you'll find an appendix. There, I share more examples of my patients' dialogues with loved ones in spirit. I've included them to give you an even broader sense of the infinite ways in which you can communicate with loved ones in spirit.

I am excited to share our story with you. It's a story of the earthly loss of a great love and the recapturing of that love in spiritual form. As you take this journey with me, I know that your life will be transformed, as mine has been. If your heart is open and your mind keen to learn, I invite you now to step with me through the gates of heaven, as I share my ongoing experiences with Jean since the night he left his body.

Sharing Our Story

CHAPTER 1

FINDING JEAN AGAIN

On the first morning of my mourning
Jean was telling me good morning!

As I lay in the hotel bed, weeping uncontrollably following my husband's death, I suddenly felt Jean's hand stroke my spine. I instantly shot bolt upright. How was it possible that Jean had just touched me? I was beyond flabbergasted.

Since I wasn't going to sleep, I decided to telephone his sisters in France and my family in America. I was so distraught that it took me hours to figure out how to dial France and the United States.

As I paged through Jean's little black phone book to figure out whom I should call, I was stunned to see that he had written down my friend Ann's number. I hadn't spoken to her in nearly a decade, and Jean wasn't friendly with her. In that moment, I sensed that Jean had known on some level that I would need to reach out to her on this night. Amazingly, Ann told me months later that Jean manifested himself to her on that evening *after* he had left his body. She said that he warned her to not swallow what she was about to eat, telling her it was too heavy for such a late hour. When he came to her, Ann thought it was odd considering that she hadn't seen or heard from either of us for years. Then, when I phoned her later that night to say that Jean had passed over, she calculated the time and realized that he was already in spirit form when he had appeared to her!

After I reached everyone, I collapsed again in a heap on the bed, where I lay trembling and crying. When the first splinters of sun pierced the room, I pulled myself from the bed.

I hadn't slept a second.

I felt like vomiting.

I was freezing and shaking.

I knew that I was in shock . . . I felt like a sleepwalker in my own living nightmare. *Would I ever wake up and discover I had been having a bad dream?*

I STUMBLED DOWN THE STAIRS and dragged myself to the hotel office. I desperately wanted to flee this country and get home. But I was stuck in Italy until I could coordinate transport of Jean's body back to the States. First I had to arrange for a funeral parlor in Rome to pick him up from the hospital, an hour and a half south of the city.

There was a lot of red tape with the U.S. Department of State in order to get his body shipped back home. I had to fight with the airlines to change my return ticket so that I could fly into New Jersey rather than New York since my father, who lives in Jersey, was going to pick me up. I was also insisting on a direct flight. I couldn't bear the thought of transfers. I'd already packed my bags. I couldn't wait to get away from this country.

The hotel staff was so kind to me, holding my hand, bringing me broth.

I sat at times with Bruno in the office. He spoke to me in Italian about his marital problems. At least I could be useful. As he spoke, I noticed that I could understand him for some odd reason. I registered the fact that since Jean's bodily death the night before, I had somehow acquired his fluency in Italian. I sensed that Jean had entered me in some miraculous way but couldn't quite grasp how this miracle was happening.

After two days, two of Jean's three sisters, Marthe and Madeleine, and Madeleine's husband, Bernard, came from France to Italy to be with me. They arrived late in the evening. We sat in the empty dining room, all of us looking pale as ghosts in the harsh fluorescent lights.

The chef prepared me a vegetable broth that night. I took one spoonful and gagged. I thought he must have spilled an entire saltshaker into the pot. I recalled Jean telling me that the French say that oversalted food means the cook is in love. What an odd thing to have remembered at that moment.

Still weeping and trembling, I haltingly described the details of Jean's death to his family.

They listened in sober silence as I reported how the hospital murdered my darling.

They were mute as mannequins in a store window.

Madeleine's mouth was a thin seam of sorrow.

She silently handed me the Valium I'd asked her to bring.

I took one at the table on an empty stomach. It made me woozy. I felt like vomiting all the more.

Later that evening, Marthe lay down in my bed and held my hand. I hadn't shared a bed with anyone but Jean for nearly 30 years. I felt comforted knowing she shared his DNA.

THE NEXT MORNING, THEY DROVE ME to the airport.

In the car, I tried to transcribe their latest home and cell phone numbers into Jean's little black address book. I was having trouble writing. I felt like a kindergartener who hadn't learned her numbers yet. I kept crossing out the marks and starting over.

When I arrived at the airport in Rome, I was terrified to see that there was only *one* check-in line for all the departures. I knew that if I went to the end of the line, I'd never make my flight.

Suddenly a woman rushed forward from very far down the line and came to me. She sensed that I was in trouble. She took me by the hand to the head of the line and got me checked in. I thanked her and she disappeared back into the crowd.

During the flight, I was astonished to discover that that very woman who helped me break the line was actually on my flight and seated just behind me! It was at this moment that I realized there are no coincidences. Coincidence is simply spirit's way of remaining anonymous.

She knelt beside me as I wept and told her my story. She held my hand and spoke lovingly to me.

She told me that she'd undergone a botched surgery and the result was she could no longer have sex. Even in my stupor of grief, I registered that Jean had sent me an angel to comfort me during the flight—and to remind me that other people may have suffering that is even worse than mine. This was the first of many experiences that showed me that our loved ones in spirit send us angels to support us during our times of difficulty.

WHEN I FINALLY ARRIVED IN NEWARK, I'd been awake for days. Stumbling forward on rubbery legs, I saw my father waiting outside the arrival gates.

There was a rabbi standing next to him.

I felt a wave of comfort. I thought, *My father brought me a man of the cloth, to help me feel closer to Jean.*

My father hugged me stiffly, then said, "Do you see that rabbi? He was trying to talk to me. I told him to get lost."

His harshness stabbed my heart. In my grief, I felt as though he were insulting Jean, who had also been a religious for most of his life.

I again felt like vomiting, to get rid of the poison. But Jean was gone. There was no way to expel that poison.

My father drove me to my mother's house and dropped me off at the curb. He didn't help me with my suitcase. He just drove off, not wanting to risk seeing his ex-wife.

THE NEXT NIGHT MY MOTHER DROVE me back to Jean's and my house. As soon as her tires crunched on our pebble drive, I was overcome with chills, shaking, and trembling. *I must have malaria of the soul,* I thought.

I entered the house and burrowed into bed. My mother gave me a Valium. I lay alone, weeping, clutching Jean's pajama top to my nose, like a little girl clinging to her favorite teddy bear. I inhaled deeply, smelling Jean's beautiful scent that always filled me with such ecstasy. I wept and wept and wept, begging to be wrapped in the arms of death.

Suddenly, as if an IV tranquilizer had been inserted in my vein, a tidal wave of peace and love entered me. My chest felt bathed in warm, golden light.

Words that were not my own began pouring into my head. At the time, I didn't know the technical name for what was happening to me. I just knew that Jean was implanting words, thoughts, and feelings into me. Jean was suddenly a voice inside my head. The voice was clearly not my own. He was in my mind.

He said, *You can't give up. You can't die. We have so much work left to do in our ministry.*

I was stunned by the message, but not afraid. "Ministry? What ministry?" I asked aloud. I didn't have a clue what he was referring to. The word *ministry* sounded daunting, especially for an atheist. Clearly he knew this wasn't the time to go into detail. He didn't say more on this point, but I sensed that he would clue me in when he felt the time was right.

Even in that moment, I knew that Jean was showing me that our loved ones in spirit are here to help us weather life's storms, assist us in completing our journey, and even guide us to fulfill our destinies. Despite registering that thought, I again wept in misery over having to live another 40 years or more on Earth without him.

I silently asked, *How do I live in the world when the entire world is gone?*

In reply, the following words popped into my mind: *You'll never be without me. Your head rests on my shoulder morning and night and whenever else you want to connect with me.*

He continued, *My arms are always open to you. What else is there for me to do? My full-time occupation is to love you . . .*

This was the first of many rhymes that I've heard from Jean. His rhymes, I soon realized, were his way of underscoring a point, to make sure I would remember his message.

He cajoled me through the night, buoying my sinking soul with words of love. *Come to me, my little darling* [his daily term of endearment for me], *whenever you need me.*

His words of reassurance reminded me that I was not alone. (Nor are you. Your loved ones are always watching over you until your days are through.)

The hours passed.

His vigil continued.

At one point, he said, *My little darling, don't be afraid of being alone in the dark. It is in the silence that you will hear my voice. The conversation and the noise of the day drown out my voice. Any time you want to talk to me, come to the bed, be still, and you will hear me. It is in the quiet that we will always unite.* He again said, *I am always available to you. I'm holding your hand every minute.*

Jean went on to tell me, *I had to go. I needed to be in the form I'm in to protect you better.* He added that he could help me better from the place where he was.

During this entire magical evening, his words poured over me like a fountain of love, a babbling brook overflowing its banks. I didn't sleep a bit. How could I? Like new lovers chatting the night away, Jean and I had found each other again. I didn't want to close my eyes. I was afraid to lose him.

CHAPTER 2

PREPARING
OUR FUNERAL

I put all my love for you in one basket
Now you're gone and in a casket
You were my husband, lover, and my best friend
From all this loss I'll never mend

The next morning, I again dragged my aching bones from bed. When I entered the kitchen, I sensed Jean urging me to open the back door. I felt no choice but to obey.

When I opened the door, I saw a chipmunk seated on the field-stone step. I stood motionless and watched him. He was still for some time, as though in a trance. Suddenly he began to choke, gasp, and rip at his face, mimicking the way Jean had tried to tear off the oxygen mask. Tears rained down my cheeks as I saw the creature re-creating Jean's death. Finally, after about a half hour of torment, the chipmunk actually coughed up some mucus and was in peace. I wept for joy over this miracle in which Jean magically materialized the mucus that the little creature expelled from his lungs. Even in my sleepless and befuddled state, I knew that Jean was speaking to me through this tiny animal, telling me that he was all right.

I vaguely registered why Jean chose to speak to me through a chipmunk—because he knew of my special love for them. Even in my grief, I realized that when spirit speaks through animals, they behave uncharacteristically. They may sit still as though in a trance, as this little friend did.

THE NEXT MORNING, I AGAIN stumbled from bed. I still hadn't slept a wink. I was so heartbroken that I could hardly breathe. The pain in my chest was excruciating. I thought I was dying. I wanted to die. I didn't want to live without my Jean.

I ran my tongue across my lips. They were parched from days of crying, parched from living in the desert that was now my life. There weren't—and aren't—enough words in the universe to say what a wonderful man Jean was and is. I felt compelled to write every detail. I knew that I didn't have enough days left in my life to say it all. First I wanted to write what happened to him in Italy, so that I wouldn't forget. I wanted to avenge his wrongful death.

Later in the day, my mother and I went to the funeral home to write Jean's obituary. Mike, the owner, asked me to bring clothing for Jean. I dithered in his closet, trying to put together a beautiful outfit. I always coordinated his shirts, ties, and jackets. I loved dressing my adorable, handsome boy. He always loved the attention. I chose a soft green silk jacket, a matching silk tie, and toasty-colored linen pants. I carried the clothing into the funeral home, clutching his earthly belongings to my heart, like a little girl clinging to her security blanket. Making these preparations, I felt as though I were getting ready to be buried as well, my life having ended with Jean's.

Mike turned on his computer and asked me to dictate Jean's death announcement—but his computer wouldn't type the notice. We tried and tried to no avail. I didn't realize at the time that this was a sign from Jean. He was telling me that he wasn't gone.

I SAT BEFORE MY COMPUTER AT 5:55 A.M. the next day, my hands resting on the keyboard as I prepared to write Jean's eulogy. I was beyond exhausted. My brain wasn't working right. I couldn't string two coherent thoughts together. Yet somehow his eulogy magically appeared on the page.

As I was writing the last line, which paraphrased Auden, I originally typed, "You *were* my north, my south, my east, and my west." With my hands resting in my lap, the word *were* kept changing to the word *are*. I kept changing *are* back to *were*. Each time, the computer changed it back again! I tried 15 times. I could hardly fathom what was happening. Was it possible that Jean was showing me that he could use whatever means possible to let me know that he wasn't gone—that he was still my compass and my world?

Later that day, Mike from the funeral parlor called. He said Jean's body finally arrived from Rome. He told me that the body hadn't been handled well—meaning there was a lot of decomposition. He said that he wouldn't be using the clothing I gave him because there would be no open casket. The thought of Jean's rotting and mangled flesh made me sick. I collapsed on my office couch, too bereft to move.

Standing in the doorway of my office, my mother said in a disgusted tone, "I had no idea how fragile you are."

Despite having endured a lifetime of put-downs from her, I still hadn't developed a thick enough skin to prevent her from wounding me. As I wept on the couch, I felt kicked when I was already facedown in the mud. I was too weak to tell her so.

LATER IN THE DAY, I HAD ARRANGED to meet with Jean's priest to discuss the readings for his funeral. My mother was frantic. She wanted me to go to the bank and open a local account in my name before I saw the priest.

I said that there wasn't time. If I went to the bank, I'd be late for the meeting with the priest.

She was furious.

"You're torturing me," I said.

"Go fuck yourself. You don't have a mother anymore," was her response.

I left the house and ran to the car, weeping pitifully.

I said aloud, "Jean, look what I'm left with. You were the angel who was sent to save me from my first family. I feel like a holocaust survivor who's lost her entire family. I was so devoted to you. You were everything to me. I just wanted to spend every minute with you. Now I pay."

I MUST SAY HERE THAT BEING with Jean was such ecstasy that time spent with others paled in comparison. Hence, I never felt the need to cultivate other deeply intimate relationships. In addition, because of our age difference, I was acutely aware of our days being numbered. This made me greedy. I didn't want to miss a moment of our precious time together.

I also must share that my mother later told me that when I fled the house, she heard a loud banging sound on the walls, like someone was angrily pounding them. This went on for a half hour until she fled the house in terror! When she later reported this to me, on Christmas Eve, I said to her, "But Mom, you don't believe in the afterlife." To which she replied, "I still don't believe. I just know what happened."

STILL SOBBING, I BARGED INTO the church. The priest was seated in a pew at the front near the altar. Ranting like a madwoman, I blurted out, "My mother just told me to go fuck myself," my words reverberating against the stone walls. I'd never met Jean's priest before. That was some introduction!

The priest crossed himself and said, "You can't speak that way in the church."

How would I have known? As I said, I was born into a Jewish household and was raised as an atheist. This was the first time that I'd entered a church apart from the ancient cathedrals that Jean and I visited when touring Europe.

The priest gestured for me to sit beside him in the pew. I then told him that Jean had spoken to me the night before. He lifted his brow in obvious skepticism. I then quoted exactly what Jean had told me: "I had to go. I needed to be in the form I'm in to protect you better."

The priest blanched, then crossed himself again. He said, "Dear God, at first I didn't believe that Jean was speaking to you, but I do now."

Apparently I was quoting the dying words of St. Dominic, which are used in the Catholic catechism to affirm the Communion of Saints. The priest didn't tell me the significance of the passage at that time, and I was too overwhelmed at that moment to ponder why Jean had shared this passage since this was the only religious material he'd ever quoted to me. It took me a year to realize that this passage would form the theoretical foundation for our new grief-therapy method. (I'll explain this further in Part II.)

In addition to reinforcing his presence to me, Jean's astonishing manifestation was, I believe, meant to revitalize the priest's faith. Up to this point, I sensed that the man had been a religious "mechanic," performing rituals without really being convinced that this spiritual stuff was true. After all, who could blame him? Belief in the existence of an afterlife is a leap of faith for most of the world. But on that day, Jean's words proved to him that his faith is founded; the afterlife is real. He wept at Jean's funeral the next day, and I was later told that he hadn't shed tears even at the funeral of his best friend. Clearly Jean reached him and revitalized his faith through me.

As I was leaving, the priest dubbed me the "perfect pagan." He said the experiences I was having with Jean have been reported in Latin American countries, where the majority of people do not receive a formal religious education, which makes them more open to spirit. At this moment, I vaguely registered that Jean never discussed religion and spiritual matters with me when he lived in physical form because he must have known on some level that I needed to be completely unindoctrinated. This way I would be open for him to channel his wisdom from the other side . . . so that he could guide me to develop our new ministry.

CHAPTER 3

THE UNFUNERAL

The day they buried you six feet under
My entire world felt cast asunder
But no matter how much I think you're gone and dead
You keep showing me you're right beside me instead!

The day of Jean's funeral was a blur. When I backed the car out of the garage, I forgot to close the door. I discovered a few days later that I was robbed during the time I was gone for the ceremony.

My sister called as many people as possible, but most of Jean's friends and relatives throughout the United States and in Europe couldn't reach us in time.

Flowers from my old friend Ann arrived at the house. The card accompanying the flowers read, "Love Never Dies." I realized months later that Jean had moved Ann not only to remind me that our love hadn't died but also to give me the title of the book that I would soon begin writing.

I vaguely recall sitting in the funeral parlor as people came to greet me. I saw their mouths moving. Their words seemed to slide off my brain unprocessed.

When I entered the church, I was worried that it wasn't full enough. I wanted the hall to be filled to the brim. I was imagining Jean's funeral like a party that I didn't want underattended. Crazy—especially since I would come to understand that this was really an *unfuneral:* not an end, but a new beginning.

I wept throughout the service. I felt out of my body. The voice of the priest sounded far away, as though I were hearing a conversation with my head underwater. I faintly heard him say that Jean and I were perfectly matched. He also mentioned the astonishing proof Jean gave of the afterlife when he quoted the catechism regarding the Communion of Saints to me. The priest described me as disconsolate.

Pat, Jean's colleague, read the famous passage from 1 Corinthians ("Love is patient, love is kind . . ."). I vaguely thought it was odd that she'd chosen a reading that's usually used for wedding ceremonies.

Then my friend Gayle walked to the lectern. She paused in front of a bouquet of red roses (not knowing that Jean always gave me a bouquet of roses each week). Even in my mental befuddlement I knew that he had moved her to remove one and carry it with her. She placed it on the podium. Then she read the eulogy I'd written. At one point, she had to stop because she was crying.

At various points during the funeral mass, I sensed movement, as the Catholic attendants rose up and down, like buoys bobbing in a sea of grief. Someone told me weeks later that the priest invited those who were in good standing with the church to receive Holy Communion. When I heard this, I was mortified that this type of exclusion had occurred at Jean's funeral service. He would not have approved.

WHEN THE SERVICE WAS OVER, I dimly remember walking behind the coffin as I exited the church. Somehow I ended up at the grave site. I recall watching them lower Jean into the ground. I couldn't seem to pull myself from the spot.

I saw my friend Ann standing opposite me, observing the scene. I knew that she would be my eyes. Constant crying had made my vision blurry. I was too overloaded to absorb what was happening around me. Ann later told me that my father put his arm around me. My mother stood stiffly off to the side. She didn't touch me. She later said that she hated my eulogy because it made her eyes "leak." She resented that, because she doesn't believe in crying.

I don't know how long I stood gazing into the gaping hole that was now to be Jean's bodily home. I wanted to be pushed into the hole with him. I couldn't move from the spot. After many silent minutes, I recall feeling a hand on my elbow. Somebody pulled me away from him.

The procession drove to our favorite local eatery for a luncheon. I didn't eat. No food could pass the egg-sized lump of grief in my throat.

My college roommate, Debbie, and her lover, Mark, drove from the Massachusetts cape. Deb had fallen in love with Mark the same week that Jean and I came together. I hadn't seen them in decades.

My father's brother, Uncle Herman, a famous doctor, drove down from Maine to attend the funeral. I recalled the way he wept at our wedding in response to Jean's having a Catholic priest include Jewish rituals in our wedding service. He loved Jean for that.

As Herman was leaving, he said, "I never knew you could write like that," referring to the eulogy. "You have a bestseller on your hands."

(I realized only later that Jean was giving me the idea to tell our story through this most unlikely vessel. When I told my uncle months later that I was writing a book about Jean's manifestations, this atheist and quintessential man of science told my father that I'd become psychotic and delusional.)

As the luncheon progressed, the talk went on.

My sister's husband, Tom, remarked that his father was surprisingly close to him after he died.

A prominent judge we knew said he had great respect for Jean and me. I remember wondering why he included me in the compliment.

Dan, my lawyer, said, "Hearing Jean's eulogy puts us all to shame. He's a tough act to follow."

All these comments washed over me. Nothing entered me. I was impervious. Dead.

Our remaining friends and colleagues left the restaurant en masse, like a flock of migratory birds.

Then my entire family fled the scene, as though they were escaping a leper colony.

In minutes, the parking lot was a ghost town.

GAYLE, WHO LIVED IN MARYLAND, came home with me. She planned to stay the night and catch a train early the next morning.

Sunday morning dawned like the last day on Earth. I wept uncontrollably. I knew that when I deposited her at the train, I would be alone for the first time in my life.

She decided to take a later train so that she could bring me with her to the monastery in West Park, New York, where she had several friends. She introduced me to the brothers. I think she was hoping that contact with them would keep me from hurling myself from the Mid-Hudson Bridge.

Afterward, I dropped her off at the train and drove home. As I entered the house, I was overcome by terror. I was shaking, shivering, and trembling again. My heart was racing. I didn't want to live. I wasn't scared to die. I yearned for it as a weary traveler craves sinking into a feather mattress.

CHAPTER 4

◇◇◇

BACK TO BUSINESS

◇◇◇

So as to not go berserk
I must pour myself into work

I returned to my office the following morning. My friend, colleague, and supervisor, Lou Ormont, encouraged me to do so, reminding me that work integrates the psyche. If that weren't sufficient incentive, I also desperately needed the money. An addition to the house had been completed right before we left for Italy. The mortgage payments alone were $6,500 per month! I couldn't imagine how I was going to pay the bills without Jean's income.

One of my patients quit during the evening group I facilitate in a nearby town. I began to tremble as soon as she made the announcement. I vaguely registered that patients would probably follow suit because they didn't want to face their feelings about death and dying.

When the group was over, I managed to get as far as my car. I stabbed the key into the ignition and burst into tears.

I drove home weeping. *How can I face all this terror alone? How will I bear another night of silence and emptiness?* I thought, *My poor adrenal glands aren't going to be able to handle this stress. How am I going to survive this? How will I manage?*

Like an overloaded circuit, my brain suddenly clicked off. The trauma was more than I could tolerate. I wasn't in my body anymore. I vaguely registered that this was an extreme anxiety reaction.

WHEN I GOT HOME, I PARKED THE CAR in the garage. As I got out, my teeth were chattering. The night was chilly, but not enough to warrant my shivering. I suddenly felt Jean urging me to look heavenward. This was the first of what would soon be many times in which my eyes felt pulled in a certain direction. Even in my haze of grief, I knew that I had to pay attention to this feeling because it was Jean's way of gently tugging me to follow his guidance. Later, I learned that what I was experiencing is called clairsentience, which is the formal name for the ability to sense spirit.

As I looked up, I saw pinpricks of starlight peeking through the moth-eaten blanket of sky. Just then a shooting star streaked the heavens. I knew that this remarkable manifestation was Jean's way of letting me know that he was with me in my suffering. To prove it, he literally moved heaven (the stars in heaven, to be exact) and earth to offer me a miraculous sign that he was, indeed, present.

DESPITE HIS ASTONISHING SIGN that night, I awoke the next morning to gut-wrenching pain. The cataclysm of Jean's death had opened a seismic gap in my soul. How would I ever fill this gaping void? Hot tears flowed like lava burning my cheeks. The aftershocks and tremors were endless, ripping new holes in me.

Even though living in silence was a torment, I felt led to discontinue the television service and sit in the stillness. It seemed I had no choice. I felt as though I were being forced to enter a silent monastic order.

So I sat; I listened; I breathed. And one day, it hit me. I was now 48, the same age that Jean had been when he left the Jesuits! I knew that it wasn't a coincidence that I was entering some type of order at the same age that Jean had left.

I was beginning to realize that my life was mimicking Jean's in the Jesuit novitiate, where he was forced to "mortify" himself by wearing instruments of penance such as belts with metal spikes that cut into his naked flesh, and by beating himself with whips made of knotted ropes. He once told me that he was always moved by beauty and prided himself on his handsome appearance. To exorcise his vanity, his beautiful hair was shorn to the scalp on the day he entered the order. Later, to further eradicate his pride, his superior forced him to put out his first book with an inferior press and reject the acceptance of the most illustrious publisher in France, which had wanted to publish his work. These mortifications were designed to tear down his ego and open his vessel to God.

I felt a similar process was happening to me, with the spirit realm, so that I could be born into our new ministry. I realized that my father's statement to me when I was young that I could be perfect mirrored the "quest for the life of perfection," the stated mission of Ignatius of Loyola, the founder of the Jesuit order. I also had a flash of insight that life in my first family also mimicked the mortification process that Jean underwent. In fact, much of my life had been a series of mortifications, which I'll discuss a bit later in the book. Finally, Jean's earthly loss culminated this process. I could feel that I was being purged and purified, to open my vessel more fully so that I could channel Jean and other spirit beings.

During this time, I also began to feel that I wasn't fully living on the earth plane. I felt weightless, as though I were floating— a description that people often used for how Jean moved. I also often misspoke and said, "When *I* died . . ."

Yet each morning I was acutely aware of not being dead when I awoke to agonizing pain in my heart, which felt as if it were hemorrhaging from a fatal slow bleed, and the sad realization that I was still alive and living without Jean.

In addition to the pain in my heart, my guts also felt as though my umbilical cord were being constantly torn out. Like a newborn, I was doubled in half from the pain of being born into widowhood . . . but I felt more like a newborn orphan that had been left to die. Yet as much as I wanted to die, my lungs continued breathing and my heart continued beating. The days, like a merciless jailor, kept dragging me off to solitary confinement as I served what felt like a life sentence without parole. But no matter how much I begged and prayed to be set free, the great warden in the sky wouldn't release me.

AND SO MY NIGHTS AND WEEKENDS dragged on and on like an endless sentence. I couldn't bear the thought of living the years that would stretch ahead without Jean.

In spite of all the pain, I had the strength and discipline to put my feelings aside and be present with my patients. But each night after work, as I locked the front door, I again sealed the lid of my coffin. I wasn't gone yet; I was just dying the slow death of living without Jean.

To complicate matters, my old house is situated on a dark country road. Mine isn't a neighborhood with friendly faces that smile and greet you as you pass. No one knew or cared whether I was dead or alive. And all the couples we had known had disappeared from my life. Most married women my age still had kids at home; all they had time for was a hurried air kiss as their ships sailed away from me. I felt shunned as my flesh seemed to rot from my bones. I was secretly dying of leprosy of the soul.

And so I existed for days on end, submerged in my endless grief. I wept till my well of tears was dry. But each day the well filled anew. More tears flowed, but they didn't end the emptiness inside me. My lips became more and more parched. Was it from crying or because I was thirsting for Jean's kiss? Oh how I missed his kiss.

In my dark despair, I was blind and deaf to Jean.

THEN, ONE MORNING I HAD TO FAX a letter to remove Jean's name from our phone line. I was told to fax a cover letter along with his death certificate. I had sent many multipage documents earlier in the day without a problem. However, each time I tried to fax his death certificate, the cover letter went through without a hitch, but the death certificate wouldn't transmit.

I tried to fax his obituary instead. The same thing happened. The cover letter faxed but the obit didn't. I tried 20 times. No dice.

Suddenly, the thought popped into my mind: *Jean is trying to tell me that he's not gone!*

The next day, I took the papers to my lawyer's office. I didn't tell the secretaries that I was having difficulties. I just asked them to please fax the documents for me.

About ten minutes later, the secretaries came out of the back office, distraught. They said that they tried 40 times to fax both the obit and the death certificate, and while the cover letter transmitted without a problem, neither of these other two documents would fax. They concluded, "Jean wants you to know that he's not gone!"

By also blocking the secretaries' transmission, Jean, I was discovering, could use third parties to prove that he was, indeed, here with me.

He was using what I soon came to refer to as Earthly Props, like machines and people, to serve as messengers to repeat what I'd heard him telling me: in this case that he was right there! He was doing this to prove to me that I was accurately interpreting his signs and messages—to encourage me to trust my newly discovered abilities.

Not being accustomed to spirit communication, I certainly needed these validations, especially in the early days. Because spirit communication is a subtle process, it's easy to miss or dismiss signs and messages that we receive. As I was discovering, it isn't like being hit by a bus, and you don't fall to the floor foaming at the mouth or begin speaking in tongues!

The next day, I again had to fax the same cover letter along with Jean's death certificate to another company. Again, the cover letter went through, but not the death certificate.

This time, I said aloud, "You keep preventing your death certificate from faxing because I keep forgetting that you're still here with me. If I promise to try to remember, will you let the death certificate go through now?"

I canceled the fax and simultaneously felt a tidal wave of love pouring into me. I dialed the number again, and the transmission went through in its entirety! I was beginning to see not only that Jean could hear me, but also that he could use an electronic device to confirm that he had heard what I said. To further prove his presence, he infused me with the same unearthly feeling of love that he often showered me with in life!

THE NEXT MORNING, I AWOKE to the smell of burning toast wafting from the kitchen. Jean often burned his toast. Through my haze of grief, I vaguely sensed that this was his gentle way of reminding me that he was there. I needed this reassurance, since that day I was to travel to my professional group in New York City for the first time since his death. In the past, I would ride the Amtrak. Today I decided to take the Metro North commuter train, to save money.

When I got to the station, the acrid stench of the public toilet burned my nostrils and made me nauseated. My brain was wrapped in a gauze of fog. I couldn't think straight.

I queued up in Grand Central Terminal to buy a ticket for my return trip, my feet shuffling forward like an animal being herded to slaughter. When it was finally my turn, I was lost. My first check had to be torn up because it was a temporary check that didn't have my address on it. Then I had to use the debit card that was tied to my new bank account, but I couldn't remember the PIN.

A man in the line began shouting at me. I was rattled and began to cry. He said in a mocking voice, "Oh great, here come the waterworks."

I was mortified. The ticket agent said, "Ignore him. He's insensitive."

I told her that my husband had just died.

"Take all the time you need," she reassured me.

I finally got the ticket and ran inside the pharmacy across the way. I went to the rear of the store and wept. A woman came up to me and asked if I was okay. I told her that I wasn't, that my husband had just died.

After I told her my story, she said, "You're going to be fine. May I hug you?"

We embraced, and I felt like a tiny craft buffeted by the stormy seas of my hiccupping sobs.

I asked her what her name was.

She smiled angelically and said, "Eve."

Then she disappeared, as if an apparition of the original mother was brought to me and then drawn back into the ether.

LATER THAT DAY, I FREAKED OUT while riding the subway. I was rummaging inside my purse and couldn't find my wallet. I thought that it must have fallen to the ground when I bought my ticket at Grand Central.

I rushed to take the next train back to the terminal. Riding back, I found the wallet in my purse after all.

At that moment, I felt my eyes being pulled to the left where a man was reading a newspaper. The headline read, "You gotta bereave."

The headline was Jean's tender reminder that into each life some tears must fall. I had to accept that even though Jean was present to me in spirit form, I must grieve the loss of him in bodily form.

CHAPTER 5

DISCOVERING HOW TO DIALOGUE

My darling, we are never apart
So please keep sharing the secrets of your heart

As I was discovering firsthand, grief is like an ongoing pileup with a Mack truck. Every time I thought I'd found solid ground, the truck barreled into me again. Each time I towed myself to the repair shop to get put back together, I was soon flattened again. I hoped to end up with some new parts to show for all these collisions.

Discovering for myself how slow the grieving process is, I realized that it's wrong for professionals to tell the bereaved that they should be done with their grief in six months. Grief is a roller-coaster ride with ups and downs. Healing takes the time that it needs to take.

While coming to understand this, I also made sure to put my grieving on a strict schedule. Each night, as soon as I was finished seeing patients, I faced my loss.

To keep me from dying of despair, I felt Jean urging me to bare my soul to him, just as I did when he lived in a body. So I bought a six-subject notebook. At every opportunity I had, I sat in silence and spilled my sorrow onto the pages.

Because the silence seemed to break my eardrums—more deafening than the loudest shouts—I spoke aloud as I wrote to him. Hearing my voice in the air helped ease my loneliness since I was, of course, accustomed to audible conversations with Jean.

At first I only spoke my own pain. But I soon discovered that writing to Jean was a form of verbal meditation. In no time, Jean's words began pouring from my pen. I didn't pause to think or reflect. Without imposition of reason or conscious thought, I just wrote. The process felt similar to free-associating. Soon, Jean was my fingers; Jean was my pen. And then Jean was guiding me to speak *his* words aloud as I wrote. Through this "automatic writing," I was discovering that we could dialogue with each other.

The next thing I knew, Jean was sharing all kinds of information about the soul's purpose on earth, the role suffering plays in soul development, fate and destiny, and the afterlife. It was clear that he wanted me to record all this and write a book on the topic, to share this wisdom with the world.

It wasn't long before I found myself speaking to Jean even when I wasn't writing in the notebook. I was talking aloud to Jean every chance I had! This was the beginning of our regular dialogues, as I was discovering that Jean and I could communicate using these Earthly Props.

As I have shown previously, spirits often use props from the material world to offer signs of their presence. These "static" signs of spirit presence can be powerful indeed, but they do not constitute a dialogue, which only occurs when animate and inanimate props are used to facilitate a nonverbal *back-and-forth* exchange between you and a spirit presence.

The props are endless. Spirits will use whatever means they can to engage in a dialogue with you. When you are outdoors, wild animals and insects are the obvious choices because they are, as I have said, Open Vessels.

When you are indoors, domestic animals (also Open Vessels) and electronic devices are commonly used.

Last but not least, humans who are Open Vessels are often selected to assist in the dialoguing process. Open Vessels of the human kind include the very young and old, the sick, the disabled, the dying, the mentally ill, the homeless, and healers. With the ability to dialogue through so many messengers, a whole new world opens up!

ONE DAY WHILE DRIVING, I felt the need to expand our dialogues and actually pray *to* Jean. I had been thinking about my friend Emily's loneliness and her desire to find a partner. So, I prayed aloud to Jean to help her find love. When I completed the prayer for her, I was instantly overtaken by a tidal wave of love that drowned me in euphoria. I just knew that this was Jean's way of acknowledging that he had heard my prayer. I looked at the clock. It was 5:45.

Later that night, Emily called me and said that a man, whom she had never met or seen in photographs, came to her at 5:45 P.M. exactly. I asked her to describe the man who appeared to her, and she perfectly described Jean! She said that at that moment she fell into a trance during which Jean told her, *To find love, follow the gray stones to the church in your neighborhood.* This made no sense to her, but she obeyed and went to the church.

Her report ended at this point. I was so stunned that I didn't ask her for further details. Jean's purpose in having her call me was to prove to me that he had heard my prayer. By appearing to her, repeating the exact wording of my prayer to him (please help her find love), and then having her report this to me was his way of closing the loop—to prove his presence beyond a doubt.

The next week, Emily told the story in our professional group. She then said where Jean had led her: the Claremont church. She hadn't told me this during our phone call.

Another member of our group exclaimed, "Oh my God, that's the only Liberation Theology seminary in New York!" As I said previously, Jean was a founder of the Liberation Theology movement! Sending my friend to *that* church, as opposed to any other, was Jean's way of putting his stamp on the miracle—to further prove that he'd heard my prayer and that he was on it. Sending her to the church was also a gift to her. Clearly, he felt that her path to love needed to begin on the spiritual level and that an earthly love wasn't what her soul most needed at this point.

Each time Jean answers my prayer for someone else, I am twice blessed. In bringing a miracle to the other person, he also reminds me of his loving presence in *my* life. In this case, by appearing to my friend and guiding her, he was proving to me that he had heard my communication to him and fulfilled my prayer!

AROUND THIS SAME TIME, I kept hearing Jean say to me, *Tell our story.* Amazingly, strangers began walking up to me and saying, "Your husband says to tell your story." I was flabbergasted since these people didn't know Jean or me, and therefore couldn't have known that I was widowed. By having so many people repeat to me what I heard him say, he was again proving his presence and further reassuring me that I was reading him accurately. At the same time, he was telling me that the sharing of our story was essential to our ministry.

During this period, several people began telling me that I was "glowing." One night, I asked Jean why that was so.

He replied, *Brides glow, Jamie. We are newlyweds in the new, spiritual phase of our relationship.*

Later that night, I was weeping, missing Jean's physical presence, when I saw an incoming e-mail from a man who had written to me a few weeks earlier to inquire about my online testimonial for a mattress that I had bought. The testimonial was posted, with my name, on the mattress company's website. I imagine the man did a search for my name and figured out how to contact me through my website. I had responded to his original e-mail saying that I did honestly like the mattress but couldn't speak further with him about it because I was newly widowed and inundated with problems. At that time, he wrote me back and said, "My little darling, my little love [Jean's exact terms of endearment!] . . . I'm so sorry."

On this night, as I wept, I received a new e-mail from this same man. The message said, "I just wanted to send you a picture of my beloved pet bird named Jamie." This by itself was remarkable since he had no way of knowing that I love birds and that Jean and I had once had a pet canary named Fluffy. I opened the photo attachment and saw his bird. Then I noticed that there was a second photo attachment. I opened it, and to my utter amazement, I was staring at a photo of the Arc de Triomphe in Paris. Where did Jean and I go on our honeymoon? Paris! And what did our hotel room overlook? The Arc de Triomphe!

I immediately wrote back to the man and asked him if he knew that he'd sent me this second photo, and, if so, why. The man didn't respond, and I never heard from him again. This led me to wonder if he was a real person or an angel. The fact that he didn't respond brought me to the possibility that he might not even exist. How Jean managed to work through an e-mail program was and is beyond my comprehension. A phenomenon that can't be understood is yet another sign that we are in the presence of the Divine, which is something that can't be fathomed by the human mind.

DURING THIS SAME PERIOD, I decided to give myself some physical comfort. So I resumed employing a massage therapist named Mark. He hardly knew me, having begun massaging me only a couple of weeks before Jean and I left for our vacation in Italy. He hadn't known Jean at all.

The first night Mark arrived at my house, he looked like a donkey carrying saddlebags. He hauled in his various supplies and set up his portable table, heating pad, and CD player in the great room of the house's new addition.

As soon as his hands touched me, I burst into tears. His touch reminded me that Jean would never touch me again. This was more than I could bear.

At that moment, the entire house was suddenly plunged into darkness.

A few seconds later, the lights came back on in the old part of the house, but they stayed off in the room we were in. The CD player stayed off as well, but the heating pad turned back on. I recalled that Jean always wanted me to be warm.

The next thing I knew, heavenly music began filtering in from the room above me. I was completely disconcerted. How could music be coming from above my head?

I reasoned that the music must have originated from the neighbors' house. I jumped off the table, stark naked, and flung the patio doors open. I listened for the music, sure that I would hear it coming from the neighbors' direction.

Then the music stopped.

I burst into tears.

This was so soon after Jean had died, and I was still discovering his powers.

When I realized that Jean was the author of these miraculous events, I said aloud, "It was you. I hurt your feelings. I didn't know you could do something like that with the music!"

At the same moment, Mark appeared to be in a trance. His eyes looked glazed over, just like the chipmunk's eyes had appeared on my first morning back home from Italy. He then began to speak words that Jean had said to me in private.

Mark said, "My little darling, my little love." Hearing him use Jean's private terms of endearment, something that Mark could have never known, confirmed that Jean was, indeed, here with me.

Mark continued, "Have faith in faith, have trust in trust, open your heart, and believe. I bring you the miracle of this music because you were the miracle of my life."

With that, the music from above turned on again.

Jean continued speaking through Mark: "You blessed my life . . . Grieve, but don't close your heart. Grieve, but I want you to find peace. Let your heart sing. Let your heart fly free, like the angel that you are. You are so gentle and kind. Never lose that."

At that moment, I fell into a trance as well. I saw a heavy planter with a tree inside it. It fell over. I stood it up again. I thought that Jean was implanting that image in my mind to let me know that I would stand up again, too.

After Mark and I had both come out of our trances, we marveled at what happened. The massage was completed without any further interruptions, and then we tiptoed upstairs to see if we could figure out where the music was coming from. There's a CD player in my sauna. That was the machine Jean had turned on and off throughout the evening! The CD called *Comfort* was still playing.

OVER THE WEEKS THAT FOLLOWED, similar phenomena occurred at each appointment, including messages that repeated word-for-word what I'd been hearing Jean tell me during our private dialogues. Out of nowhere Mark said, "What makes you think that the realm where you are isn't the illusion and the realm where I am isn't the reality?"

This blew my mind. Hearing Mark repeat what I'd heard Jean tell me—that the realm he's in *is* the reality—was beyond belief. Jean was reiterating to me that his realm is where we began and where we return and that our earthly ride is apparently like a waking dream, a place where we're meant to learn and grow in preparation for eternal life in the afterlife, when we will reunite with God, the saints, and our loved ones. It was also in this moment that I received the understanding of why we avoid loving fully: because losing a loved one is so painful. To protect ourselves, we psychologically keep one emotional foot out the door. Since Jean's messages and manifestations were proving that we don't lose those we love, I knew in this moment that we have no reason to resist loving others with all our hearts. We must leap off the ledge of love knowing that death ends a physical life, not a relationship.

THE WEEK AFTER THE MUSIC INCIDENT, I could hardly wait to see Mark. I sensed that Jean wanted to speak to me and touch me through him.

Sure enough, Mark took my hand and said, "Death is an illusion, Jamie. There is a very thin veil between the realm where you are and the realm where I am. I'm standing right here. I'm holding your hand every minute." Mark was again reiterating the messages that Jean had told me, again proving to me that I had heard him accurately!

In that moment, I smelled Jean's scent—the pièce de résistance that underscored his presence. I again wept in joy.

Jean went on to have Mark repeat more specific details about the afterlife that I had also previously heard Jean tell me. I will share some of these details with you in Part II to help you move past any mainstream misconceptions and beliefs that may create obstacles to your own reconnection.

After this massage, Mark phoned me on his way home. He said that Jean had asked him to call me and describe what had been happening since our first session. He said that for the past six weeks, as he drove home, he'd had to pull over because he was literally "choking on loogies." He said that each time he had to expel thick mucus from his throat.

How was it possible that Jean was able to generate a productive cough in Mark? I was floored. Amazingly, after Mark revealed this to me, he never choked again.

This astonishing manifestation was Jean's way of proving that his spirit had, indeed, entered Mark's body and created the same manifestation that I had witnessed with the chipmunk. In addition to Jean yet again proving his presence to me, I briefly wondered if he had used the chipmunk and Mark's bodily vessel to help him clear the trauma of suffocating to death.

As Jean was teaching me, now that his spirit was no longer contained in a physical vessel, he was able to move about freely and enter other Open Vessels in ways that weren't possible when he lived in a body.

And I was also realizing that when Jean enters animals and people's bodies, he is able to move them to love me in his name.

THE NEXT DAY, I WENT TO SPEAK with Jean's priest. I was excited to share with him what had been happening with Mark.

The priest told me, "Be prepared. When Jean enters heaven, his manifestations will stop and you will only find him again when you are reunited in heaven."

All day I was so bothered by what the priest had told me. Then I heard Jean say, *Heaven is a state, Jamie, not a place. Where would I go? I have nowhere to go but to be with you. My full-time occupation is to love you.*

Later that day, I was in my office about to start a group. A new patient of mine named Ashley was the first to arrive. She didn't know Jean or me at all, and she certainly didn't know that I was widowed. As we waited for the other members to arrive, we heard the chiming sound that my security system emits when the front door is opened. Then we heard loud footsteps. The footsteps stopped in the waiting room outside my group room.

I said to Ashley, "It must be another patient who got his appointment time wrong."

At that moment, we heard the footsteps once again. This time, they sounded as if they were leaving. I jumped up and opened the door to the waiting room, to speak to the patient. There was no one there.

Then, I went to the front door and opened it. There was no human being outside and no parked car. My house, where my office is located, has a very long driveway. No one could have had the time to reach his car and drive off in these few seconds. I registered that this was Jean's answer to the priest's erroneous statement that once Jean was in heaven, I would no longer hear from him. I returned to the group room. I told my patient there was no one outside, and she responded, "It was a spirit."

At that moment, Jean proved to me yet again that he is not only present but totally aware of whatever troubles me—verifying again that our loved ones in spirit are sentient beings that know our thoughts, feelings, and concerns.

LATER THAT WEEK, MY FRIEND ANN was scheduled to take me to dinner. I had a fleeting thought that dining with her would feel like Jean was "coming home" to me because I sensed that she, too, would be open enough to allow Jean to speak through her.

The moment she arrived, she blurted out, "Honey, I'm home!" She immediately clapped a hand over her mouth, mortified to have said something so crass.

I told her not to worry; she was simply speaking Jean's words. He was using her to let me know that he had heard my thought that he was coming home to me!

Later at the dinner table, Ann, who isn't demonstrative in the slightest, suddenly had tears in her eyes. She said, "I wish I had a camera to capture your beauty tonight."

I was astounded and instantly began crying myself. Only I knew that when we dined out, Jean had often said those very words to me—and with tears in *his* eyes.

At that moment, I asked Ann if she knew what she'd just said. She didn't. In fact, she looked as if she were in a trance. Her eyes had a faraway, glazed expression. Ann explained to me that she'd felt a gentle nudge, as though she was being pushed aside; then, she felt pressure to blurt out words that weren't her own.

Jean was showing me again that loved ones in spirit will validate their presence by implanting into an Open Vessel a message that is highly personal, something that only you and your loved one would find meaningful. In this case, *I wish I had a camera to capture your beauty tonight* are words that Ann would have never known to use had she not been informed by Jean's spirit. This process, incidentally, lies at the core of a medium's interaction with a spirit.

In my heart, I knew in this moment that this experience should not be confused with demonic possession. It was clear that Jean had no wish to violate or force another person to say or do something that was utterly against his or her will. Rather, I could see that he was choosing to speak through those who were open and willing to be used in the service of love.

Despite all Jean's signs and manifestations, I am ashamed to admit that I found it hard to hold on to his presence. *Am I just missing him in human form? Or is there something seriously wrong with me?* I wondered.

As I lay in bed one night, missing him terribly, I covered my face with his pajama top and inhaled his scent deeply.

Then I heard Jean say, *Breathe my scent into your pores. I am here.*

I suddenly felt a rush of love and sexual ecstasy filling me.

He continued, *Breathe deeply and draw my soul inside your body, my love. Whenever you want to connect with me, use the breath to draw me inside your body.*

Jean was now showing me that, in addition to being still and quiet, breathing deeply enables us to connect with spirit. In Part II, I will show you exactly how to use your breath to help you reconnect with spirit.

The following morning, Ann called. I was utterly astonished when she said, "Last night I felt Jean permeating every cell of your body, and then I saw your bodies fusing as one!"

I couldn't believe that she was describing our union of the night before. At the same time, I was becoming familiar with the way Jean was now routinely using others—anyone who was open enough—to repeat his messages to me, to reinforce his presence, and to solidify my own confidence in my mediumistic abilities.

The next morning, as I awoke and drifted back to consciousness, I became aware that my heart was hurting less since Jean had come to me that night. When I was fully awake, I heard a creaking sound on the floorboard outside the bedroom door. I could hardly believe my ears! When Jean lived in a body, I often heard this sound in the morning as he tiptoed past our bedroom door in order to not awaken me. I have heard that creaking sound many mornings since.

DURING THIS PERIOD, I WAS NOT sleeping well, even with prescription sleeping pills. Ann had been spending three nights a week at my house, so I wouldn't be constantly alone.

One morning, I was so tired and crying so desperately that she put me back in bed.

She touched my arm and said, "Jean wasn't blowing smoke. Your skin is so soft." She went on, "Rest your bones now."

After she left the room, I felt a strong weight pressing me down into the bed. It felt like Jean was lying on top of me.

This was the second time that Jean made me aware of his presence by inducing the sensation that he was touching me. The first time this occurred was the night he left his body when I felt his hand stroke my spine.

On this occasion, I felt his weight upon me and then felt that familiar tidal wave of love entering me from head to toe.

He asked, *Can you feel me holding you, my love?*

I answered, "Promise you'll never leave me."

As if I could . . .

I felt a wave of peace and joy, a drugged sleepiness, like after sex.

He then said, *Lie with me now and sleep.*

I slept for nearly two hours, feeling his presence beside me even then. As I slept, he embraced me with such passion. His arms wound tightly around me. He pressed himself against my womb, exactly as he did when he hugged me in life. When he used to embrace me like that, I'd always laugh and say, "There's gravy in that hug."

He kissed my lips passionately.

I heard him clear his throat as he did often in life.

I saw his cleft chin.

An imaginary camera circled the scene, capturing every aspect, angle, and detail.

He spoke words of love to me. He told me he was giving me all of himself and more, even more than he did in life.

Then, I awoke.

I realized at that moment that when my conscious mind is asleep, I'm even more receptive to spirit. There was no question that Jean had just been with me—the experience felt nothing like an ordinary dream state. While dreams are often disjointed, this visit was a cohesive experience. It felt as if Jean had entered my psyche and preempted my sleep with the announcement: "We interrupt this broadcast . . ." I also noticed that the experience was lifelike and vividly detailed to the point of being superreal. It actually seemed in Technicolor.

Jean's visit bathed my heart in an anesthetic balm. For the moment, I was calm.

SOON AFTERWARD I TRAVELED to Connecticut to meet with my new writers' group. The members were now becoming familiar with my remarkable stories of Jean's manifestations. Gabe, an atheist and the head of the group, was particularly fascinated by my stories involving Ann. I will share more details about the following incident with Ann a little later, but for now, I'll just relate that one day I was weeping on the floor of my walk-in closet, thinking that I had to call Ann, but I didn't want to bother her during her work-day. After a half hour of crying, I heard the phone ring.

I forced myself to get up and answer the call. It was Ann!

"Did you call?" she asked.

"No," I replied. "I was busy crying on the floor of my closet."

She said, "Jamie, my phone rang and your name and number appeared on the caller ID!"

When I told the story to my writers' group, Gabe said, in a voice full of skepticism, "I'd like to see this trick repeated. And this time I'd like to see whether your phone shows a record of dialing the person without your having placed the call yourself."

Used to his doubts, I promptly forgot about this "challenge."

The following month, I was driving behind Gabe and his wife, en route to the restaurant where we were meeting for dinner.

Suddenly, I felt that tsunami of love that signals Jean's pres-ence. I glanced at the car clock and saw that it was 4:58.

When I arrived at the restaurant, Gabe jumped out of his car and ran up to me. Excitedly he said, "Jamie, you won't believe what just happened. At 4:58 my phone rang. A man's voice asked, 'Is Jamie there? Is Jamie there?'" He added that the voice had an ac-cent that prolonged the word *there*. Jean had a pronounced French accent and he did prolong the word *there*!

Gabe said, "It wasn't a real call. The voice faded away and the call never clicked off. Go get your phone and see if it dialed me at 4:58."

I dug into the bottom of my purse and retrieved the phone, and, sure enough, it had called Gabe at exactly 4:58!

I knew that this over-the-top example was Jean's way of letting us all know that our loved ones are thoroughly aware of what's going on in our lives—including our funny and serious challenges —and sharing our fears, sorrows, and joys.

CHAPTER 6

DIALOGUING TO HEAL OUR UNFINISHED BUSINESS

I am so sorry that I caused you pain
Please allow my love to remove the stain

Despite Jean's extraordinary manifestations in these months, my peace was often short-lived. Out of nowhere, phantoms leapt from the dark alleys of my psyche to ambush me and torment me with guilt. I blamed myself for being hurt and angry over what he called his "fatal flaw."

In a nutshell, as Jean aged, he grew more and more apprehensive when I wanted to connect with him either emotionally or sexually. He would freeze like a deer in headlights, and then escape by pushing me away in one way or another. I was crushed by his rejections, and as time went on I broached the subject less and less to avoid the inevitable letdown. In turn, when Jean approached me for the same reason, I found myself less able to respond.

Because we adored each other, we were frustrated, baffled, and bereft by this impasse. Jean was so capable of love, connection, and intimacy when he initiated it. So why was it not all right when I did? We sensed that the problem had to do in part with his mother (no surprise, given the lasting influence of our "deformative" years!), who was extremely invasive and controlling. She micromanaged him as a child and manipulated him terribly.

For example, she told him when he was only two that if he wanted to be her "little love," he must always obey her. As a result, he never felt secure. In an attempt to ensure her affection, he subjected himself to her will and always did her bidding. Ultimately, although he had no heart for it, he entered the priesthood because he knew it was what she wanted.

We had always assumed that when I tried to initiate sex, he was unconsciously seeing his controlling mother. His only recourse was to run for cover to avoid engulfment. Rejecting me was simply a primitive act of self-preservation.

By the last year of his life, I had learned not to take his rejections personally. I was able to tell him what his mother never did, that he could have his freedom and come to me when he felt ready. This was a deeply healing experience for him. Knowing that he was free at last from his mother's unrelenting control enabled him to feel less frightened and more able to welcome me with open arms when I did approach him.

DURING THAT LAST TRIP TO ITALY, I was suffering from a serious case of Lyme disease and was in an irritable mood. We were dining at Torre Truglia, a medieval tower with an outdoor deck overlooking the Sperlonga bay.

At dinner, Jean told me that he loved me with all his heart. Love swelled within me. I told him that the door to my heart had opened, and I asked him if we could continue talking as lovers do. I said that he could open my heart even more if he made love to me with his words. He agreed, but then fell silent. I waited the entire meal, and when I realized that he wasn't going to say anything further, I became hurt and angry. We argued and went to bed.

The next morning, I was still upset. While I sat alone on the beach, he came to me and asked me to forgive him. He said that what he thought I meant was for him to make love to me with words at some future time.

It was then, as we were conducting a postmortem of the argument, that the bee mortally wounded him. When it did, I had the oddest sensation of my own life passing before my eyes, as often happens when our own death is imminent.

In the moments that followed, time seemed to stand still. I recalled that three years earlier in Sperlonga we were nearly struck by lightning. To me, that near miss was an omen that foretold the "bolt of lightning" that had now hit Jean. I thought that it was no coincidence that lightning had struck our rose arbor before we left for vacation or that I was born three months early as a result of shock following a lightning strike to my grandparents' house, where my parents were living, leaving broken glass and blood in its wake.

After my flash of lucidity, we returned to the hotel room, as I mentioned in the Preface. It was while I was giving him the massage that Jean said he had a shattering realization about another reason why he rejected me when I approached him in a loving way.

In France, his niece had given him a book entitled *Apprendre à Vivre,* and he had just read a passage in it that spoke directly to him. He realized that his rejection of me was connected to his fear of death. He told me that he was worried that he might die without our affairs being in order. He had an irrational fear that responding to my request for emotional or sexual connection left him feeling out of control. He said that once he had the chance to complete our daily financial business and bookkeeping, he felt less worried and therefore more able to let down his guard and come to me. So, in short, fear of death had been a culprit, along with his dominating mother.

I assured him that I understood what he was telling me, and we made peace. And I *did* understand. To the unconscious mind, money symbolizes survival; lack of money symbolizes death.

Jean's fear of our financial world crumbling was a defense against his fear of impending death.

ESPECIALLY IN THE FIRST FEW MONTHS following Jean's leaving his body, I found myself caught in an insidious web of self-blame—the demonic aftershock of grief. My internal monologue raged on: *I deserved to lose you. You're lucky to be rid of me . . .* Then I heard the question *Why are you berating yourself?*

Suddenly, the answer was revealed to me. Death is the ultimate reminder of how little control we have in life. Self-blame helps us regain a semblance of control. I recall my grandmother blaming herself for months after her brother died because she declined his request to visit her. After he died, she kept saying that if only she had let him come to see her he wouldn't have died. The idea that she could have saved him was, of course, a fantasy, one that is rooted in the illusion that she actually had the power to control whether he lived or died. Believing that we have such control makes us feel less frightened. But buying into the illusion that we have it makes us vulnerable to self-recrimination: *I could have saved him but I didn't.*

As a shrink, I know that self-incrimination following the death of a loved one can also be caused by buried unconscious resentment. Most adults retain some degree of the magical thinking of childhood. Because a young child's mind doesn't separate feelings from outcomes, he or she believes that wishing Mommy or Daddy would die is the same as killing them. Since a child needs parents, it becomes dangerous to be angry with them. I recall a patient who wished that her grandfather, who had cancer, would die because he smelled odd. When he died, she had a breakdown because she thought her wish had killed him.

When we self-incriminate after someone dies, we're actually blaming ourselves for the anger we harbored, and perhaps on a deeper level even holding ourselves responsible for that person's death.

AS MY OWN SELF-INCRIMINATION barreled on like a runaway train, Jean interrupted my thoughts, midsentence. He said, *If I had known I could be so close to you from the eternity* [his term for the hereafter], *I wouldn't have had to push you away. I was holding you off because I was afraid that you would die of a broken heart after I died.*

His words shattered me. He was telling me that the fear—reacting like a deer in headlights, the rebuffs and rejections—ultimately stemmed from such depth of love we shared that it made him afraid to leave me. His distancing behavior was an unconscious attempt to create emotional space between us, in a vain effort to protect me from dying of despair. Because even he, one of the world's true mystics, didn't know that he could be so close to me in spirit form.

What we struggled with before is no longer an issue, he added, meaning he no longer needed to separate himself from me in order to protect me from the devastation of loss.

I burst into tears. What a gift he gave me in revealing that he could be even closer to me in spirit than when he lived in the physical world.

But a few days later, I couldn't shake the lingering fear that Jean's tendency to pull back was induced by me, that he may have been recoiling from me to protect himself from the abandoned infant that lives within me—to protect himself from a terminal case of chafed nipples!

As I again started doubting whether I could ever again bond with anything other than a bagel, I felt Jean leading me to his filing cabinet. He led me to a folder where I found a letter he had written to a shaman—a priest-doctor who was one of many people we consulted to help us deal with his pattern of rejecting me. In this letter, Jean wrote that the problem we had was his. He explained that he often recoiled when I approached him, out of fear that he would be devoured by my love. He stated further that he knew intellectually that his fears were irrational and that each time he had the courage to speak to me and ask for space, rather than reject me outright, I was always loving and accepting and happy to give him what he needed. His letter was a priceless gift. He was telling me in no uncertain terms that it wasn't my fault that he had rejected me and that I must no longer doubt myself. It was the final nail in the coffin of all my self-doubts on that subject.

As my experience with Jean demonstrates, sometimes we have to wait until after someone dies before a conflict can be resolved. This in turn means we must never give up hope of healing a relationship with someone who has passed.

Just as he did in life, Jean continued to bless me with his grace, kindness, and unending love.

CHAPTER 7

DIALOGUING TO HEAL MY PHYSICAL BODY

You will no longer feel so shoddy
Let me heal your physical body

After Jean helped us bring peace to what I had thought was an unresolved relationship issue (when, in fact, our issue was nothing more than profound love and the fear of being parted), his next order of business was to heal *me*.

One morning as I entered the kitchen, I heard Jean say, *I'm turning your hair brown again.*

Mind you, my hair had been flecked with gray for years, the temples being the grayest of all. I promptly launched into my first argument with Jean in spirit form! I said aloud, "This isn't possible. Once the pigment is lost, it's lost."

Jean said in his typically impish fashion, *You'll see, Jamie.*

He was so adamant on this point that I shut up and let him think that he'd won our first spiritual argument.

A couple of days later, as I was rinsing my face, I glanced up at my reflection in the mirror. To my astonishment, my hair was *totally brown!*

I was stunned beyond all imagining.

He said, *I bring you this miracle so you can see the power I have in your life.*

I wept over the beauty of his manifestation. Then I jokingly thought, *Well, he could single-handedly put Clairol out of business!*

A couple of days after that, I went to the salon for my monthly haircut with my stylist, Stacie. She took one look at me and asked, "What did you do to your hair? Have you been two-timing me?" Then she said, "Seriously, a hairdresser can tell when hair is colored or not. Your hair isn't colored. What happened?"

I told her what had transpired. She was floored.

As an aside, after a couple of years my hair started turning gray again. At that time, I asked Jean why he gave me this gift and then took it away. He replied, *I gave you this gift to prove the power I have in your life. But I didn't want to stop your aging process. Otherwise, you'd never return to me.*

AND THE PHYSICAL MIRACLES KEPT on coming. Standing in the kitchen another morning, I heard Jean again say what he told me the first night I heard him speak, but this time he expanded the message: *I now have the power to fix your metabolic disorder. I'm rebirthing you.*

I must digress to explain what Jean meant regarding my metabolic disorder. For most of my adult life, to my great despair, I weighed nearly 300 pounds. Being such a highly disciplined and—I'm ashamed to say—vain person, it was agony for me to be trapped in a body that in no way represented who I am. I often wept in despair as strangers called out to me in the street and then mooed at me or told me to go to a fat farm. Jean saw what I ate and said to me that I was more austere in my dietary habits than any monk he'd known. He sometimes joked that I ate like a rabbit, because I did.

Jean knew that my being fat was the torment of my life. When we fell in love, I was a tiny little thing—an actress, singer, and dancer who weighed 104 pounds and wore a size four. My weight problem abruptly began when my parents disinherited me early in my relationship with Jean. The cutoff was actually the result of their crumbling marriage. They were employing the scapegoating tactic they'd always used to create a tenuous bond by uniting around a target, which was always me. The emotional shock of being cut off financially, combined with the stress of working day and night to pay for my graduate studies, was more than my body could bear. It caused something to snap inside me. And in a few short months, I ballooned to 300 pounds, not having changed anything in my diet or exercise habits.

Doctors and endocrinologists couldn't figure out what was going on. They didn't believe me when I told them I hardly ate. One said, "Anyone who wants to can lose weight." Another said, "The only reason a person is fat is because she eats more calories than her body needs." How wrong he was.

Jean attended all my doctor visits and confirmed that he watched how I ate: like an anorexic. Of course no one wanted to believe it, because this meant accepting that our bodily functions can be beyond our control. Nobody likes such an anxiety-provoking thought!

One endocrinologist asked me, "Have you always had such a fat stomach?" I was stunned into speechlessness. After the fact, I wished I'd had the presence of mind to say, "Actually, when I was 104 pounds, my gut was 1,000 times fatter than it is now. Duh!"

Since doctors couldn't seem to help me, my life became a healing quest in which I experimented with almost every technique and substance known to man—or woman. I became an alternative-health specialist. My accumulated knowledge led me to offer on my website an alternative-healing encyclopedia called the Wellness Dictionary. My knowledge enabled me to help my patients resolve all kinds of health issues. It also helped me to nip in the bud any problem Jean ever had.

Because I've made it my personal mission to access my emotional core and to help others do the same, I used this same approach when addressing my health issues. I just had to find the underlying, core factors causing my weight problem. Since I don't agree with the Western method of addressing emotional and health problems (to mask the problem with drugs rather than identify the real cause), I kept researching on my own and seeing alternative doctors.

I did craniosacral therapy, acupuncture, acupressure, biofeedback, chelation therapy, IV vitamin C therapy, Reiki, Rolfing, yoga, embodiment, various forms of massage, NET, NAET, EFT, and on and on. I was poked and prodded; sprinkled with holy water; spit on; and taken on healing journeys, exorcisms, and past-life regressions with channelers and shamans. I did meditations and incantations, and had my chakras balanced and my filthy auras cleansed (as well as my pockets). In addition to all the therapies, I tried every kind of dietary regime, including no-fat, high-fat, and no-carb diets. And, for 20 years, I eliminated most foods from my diet, including wheat, grains, dairy, eggs, yeast, and sugar. What I did eat, I rotated. In addition, I fasted often. One time, I did a 10-month green-juice fast in which I ate no solid food. None of these dietary restrictions resulted in any weight loss.

I eventually discovered that my weight problem could be traced to having been born three months early. Missing the third trimester of development meant that the endocrine and neurological systems hadn't completed their formation. This created a congenital neuroendocrine weakness in me. This finally explained why the stress of my parents' cutting me off was more than my underdeveloped adrenal glands could bear. Because my neurological and endocrine systems weren't fully formed, I wasn't able to handle a lot of the stresses that others take in stride. The weight problem was apparently due to the adrenals not working properly in the face of the extreme stress of the cutoff. This caused my body to retain massive amounts of water. Some practitioners theorized that the water retention was a type of protection, a primitive way of re-creating the womb that I had lost too soon.

I spent my adult life trying to restore my adrenals and lose weight, but because I was battling a congenital problem, every *earthly* effort proved impossible. I never gave up trying to solve the problem, but no matter what treatment plan, exercise, or diet regimen I tried, nothing worked.

Finally, it was clear that nothing short of a miracle was going to help me.

JEAN KNEW THAT I WAS DEEPLY TROUBLED by my weight. One day in the early '80s, when the problem began, Jean had a vision of my weight melting away. I asked him when this would occur. He said that he didn't know.

Decades later, on the day we left for Italy, he said that he again had the vision of my weight melting away.

"When?" I again asked, pleading.

"Soon," he replied. "Very soon."

So there I was, not long after his bodily departure, and Jean was letting me know that he'd needed to be in spirit form to have the power to fix my metabolic disorder!

A couple of nights later, as I lay in bed, again holding his pajama top to my nose, he said, *Breathe my scent into every cell of your body. Make us one for eternity . . . I'm giving you my metabolism.*

The next morning, I began to feel an alarming sense of fire burning at the center of my solar plexus. It wasn't heartburn. What I felt was an intense heat. I was shocked and a little scared.

Around this time, a priest named Father Fador told me that the Holy Spirit is often depicted as tongues of fire. I certainly was feeling on fire.

Then Jean led me to find the love note that he had written to me on September 17 all those years ago, in which he said that he'd left his wife and was free to be with me. In that note, he described me as a "fire in [his] belly." I realized that he was drawing my attention to the fact that he, who was one with spirit, was familiar with the sensation of the fire of spirit in his belly. Now, I was feeling him igniting that same burning within me!

TO EXPLAIN THE NEXT PHYSICAL MIRACLE, I have to backtrack for a moment. When Jean lived in a body, every night in winter he would perform the same adorable ritual. First he burrowed under the covers and waited a couple of seconds until the feather comforter had warmed him. Then, knowing how much I adored his scent, he'd say with a sweet smile as he unbuttoned his pajama top, "I tried to not wash all my smell away."

Then, I, like a truffle pig, would burrow my nose into his armpit. Inhaling his scent always filled me with rapture. I feigned fainting away from ecstasy. It was hardly an act. He would always roll his eyes, marveling over my passion for him.

I wasn't the only one who had noticed his amazing scent. A female neighbor once remarked to me that she couldn't believe how sexy he smelled.

A few months after Jean left his body, I noticed that his scent was dying away from his clothing. In desperation I sniffed each jacket and shirt in his closet. I finally couldn't detect his scent on anything.

When his last shirt had lost even the faintest odor, I asked, jokingly, if he could make me smell like him.

A couple of nights later, when I undressed for the evening, I noticed an unfamiliar scent coming off my body. Could it be? Was I mistaken? No! I smelled like Jean!

Now I knew for sure that something miraculous was happening to me. For my body to feel on fire and for my own odor to change meant something drastic was shifting in my entire metabolic system.

At the same time, I started feeling ravenous, as if my metabolism was on overdrive. I was starving all the time and couldn't eat enough. That's exactly how Jean described feeling. I'd heard that spirits vibrate at a very high frequency—"revved up," so to speak. I realized that because Jean lived largely in spirit, even when he was on earth, he'd already been vibrating at this very high level. Oddly, when he lived in a body, he and I had the exact same cholesterol level. But he ate butter, like a true Frenchman, while I stuck to olive oil.

It was during this time when I was feeling on fire and ravenous that I went to see my internist. When my blood tests came back, he was shocked to see that my triglycerides had suddenly become "dangerously low." He said, "You need to eat more saturated fat. I mean butter and cream and cheese."

I was starting to get the message that Jean had, indeed, given me his metabolism!

I swear on my life, I changed nothing in my eating or exercise habits to try to lose weight. But in a very short while, Jean's premonition of 30 years prior, in which he saw me melting, came to pass. In a couple of months, I went from being 300 pounds to my former size four. I was literally a fraction of my former size! Jean had given me the ultimate gift—a true miracle, considering my history. The fire of his love had entered me and burned away all my water retention.

Clearly, Jean's gift was not for me alone. It's a gift to the world because through this miracle he proves that the spirit does, indeed, live on. Freed from the vessel of the body, our loved ones in spirit have great power—more power than when they lived in this plane—to assist us in miraculous ways.

I relished this gift. It lifted my spirits and made me know Jean's presence in a palpable way . . . until things shifted once more.

CHAPTER 8

Dialoguing to Remove Obstacles to Our Ministry

Any obstacles to our ministry
Must become history!

One morning, I had a dream that I was holding Agneau, my dear little toy poodle from childhood, when my foot got caught in a large hole in the floorboards. I tripped and dropped the dog down the hole. She fell to the basement and lay in a dead heap on the floor. In agony, I grabbed a ladder and climbed down to get her—but she was gone. In her place was a butterfly. I then turned crying to my father, begging for him to see the beautiful butterfly, but he was blind.

In moments of silent self-reflection, I was becoming more and more aware of a force that was preventing me from soaring to the heights that I knew I was destined to reach. For my entire life, I'd been plagued by an internal voice that beat me down. It chanted in the background of my psyche, like the steady staccato of a drumbeat. It crushed me like an elephant squashing a mosquito. It was my father.

It is with great reluctance that I share the following personal information. I don't want to embarrass my parents, but at the same time, I feel it's important to share the details of my journey with you in the hope that my disclosures may assist you in your own healing.

Since Jean's death, I'd been grateful that my father had been kinder to me. He invited me to his home, took me out to dinner, and periodically phoned to check up on me.

At the same time, I could observe his restraining himself from being cruel to me. I often saw his lip quivering as if he were sharpening the blade of his tongue in preparation for stabbing me verbally. I was frightened that my reprieve would soon end.

I always loved my dad. One time after Jean died, I put my hand to his heart and told him so. He was frozen like a statue. He couldn't respond.

I UNDERSTOOD MY FATHER'S LIMITATIONS. His own dad was brutal to him. He was judgmental and put him down, wounding his psyche irreparably. My dad's psychic scar tissue took the form of an over-confident veneer. But festering beneath the surface is a man who's very angry and insecure.

He recounted that one day when he was young and fighting with his brother, he sank his teeth into his brother's flesh and didn't let go until he'd removed a chunk of his brother's arm that had to be sewn back. He told me proudly that as a kid he beat to a pulp—using a baseball bat—a poor neighborhood dog that had been bothering him. I also heard that in his college freshman psych class, the teacher asked the students what they'd do if they were walking in the woods and came upon an abandoned infant. My father said, "I would eat it." The teacher approached him after class and suggested that he get therapy. He didn't.

Not surprisingly, my dad had always been critical of me, putting me down and mocking me. From my earliest memories, I was beaten down and made to feel stupid. I recall writing a story in kindergarten entitled "Why Is Everyone Always Picking on Me?"

Despite being a good student and a child who excelled at my hobbies, I was never given a word of praise. Instead I was told, "Shoot for the stars" and "You can be perfect."

I so wanted to please my father and win his love and approval that I did, indeed, try to be perfect. But, of course, this was a formula for failure since no human can achieve perfection. I never heard, "Nice try." I was always told what I did wrong and what was wrong with me. It took me decades to understand that I was being used as an emotional step stool. I was being torn down so that he could build up his eroded ego.

Another way he built himself up was by turning my mother against me, then coming to my aid so that he could be the favorite parent. One day he said yes to my request to study ballet. Then he complained behind the scenes to my mother that my hobby cost too much. He got her so worked up that she came to me and pulled the plug. I hated her for it, and he came up smelling like a rose, since he was innocent and my mother was the one depriving me.

Since they were always at odds, he could achieve a reprieve in their warfare by punishing me to prove his loyalty to her. I'll never forget the day she called him to come home from work to beat me. I was between two and three years old. I hid cowering beneath their bed, knowing my mother's pregnant stomach was too large for her to reach me. My father dragged me out and told me to go up to my bedroom and wait for him. I trembled in anticipation of the beating that was soon to come.

Before every beating, he'd lay me over his knee. Then with a rough yank, he'd pull down my pants and underwear so that I would be lying naked, feeling utterly exposed and humiliated.

At this point he'd say, "I'm going to hit you so hard you're going to see lightning for a month." These words filled me with terror. And when I felt the searing blow of his hand on my soft little behind, and I heard the crack as his hand hit my flesh, I actually thought he had the magical power to bring down a bolt from the sky. The marks that were left behind were proof to me that I had been struck by lightning. When I told Jean this story, he wept and begged me to never tell him again, because he couldn't bear it.

As a kid, I never knew what to expect from my father. There were times when he could be exceedingly kind. When the angry monster that dwelled within was asleep, he played with me or made me "special grilled cheese." I even recall his patting my leg when I cried after having been given a huge injection in my thigh prior to surgery.

Each time he went after me, I sensed that he was blind with rage at his father who bullied him. This time around he would rewrite his script; this time he wouldn't be weak and helpless. Instead, *he* would be the bully venting his fury. I think he was also taking out his rage toward my mother on me, because I physically reminded him of her.

Many years later, when my parents' marriage was on its last leg, my father shot off his last flare by uniting with my mother against me in a final unconscious attempt to bring the two of them together. He wrote to me and told me everything that was wrong with me since day one. He concluded by telling me that he was cutting me off financially, the way he should have done long ago. As I said earlier, this was the blow that triggered my massive weight gain.

THROUGHOUT MY ADULT LIFE, whenever I was in my father's presence, I braced for the inevitable character assassinations. Whenever I stated an opinion, he barked, "That's wrong," or "That's not logical," or "That's not scientific."

In order to avoid the put-downs, I stopped talking about anything of significance in his presence, so he took to setting me up. He'd pose a question, and when I'd answer, he would knock me down for failing his quiz.

From time to time I asked him to accept our differences and not put me down for what I thought. He consistently refused to respond to my request and just told me that I was too sensitive. As an adaptation, I learned to walk on eggshells around him, to not say what I thought in order to avoid his attacks.

In spite of all my efforts to heal, I always labored under a "less than" feeling. This bled into every waking experience. No matter how much I achieved, it wasn't enough. I constantly compared myself to others who were accomplishing more, and felt like a failure. I always anticipated defeat and expected to be crushed by others who would succeed in ways that I never could. It was as if I transformed the entire world into him.

But, as I said, since Jean's departure, I'd felt my father resisting talking to me the way he always had. He stopped mocking me for eating organic foods, for fasting, and for the supplements I take.

In the back of my mind, however, I began to fear what would happen when he found out about my new ministry. Since he mocked religion and spirituality, I knew that I'd be in trouble if he ever found out about my experiences with Jean in spirit form. So I hid this most important aspect of myself in order to avoid the inevitable beat down.

THE WEEK BEFORE THANKSGIVING, I had prayed to Jean to help me remove any obstacles to our new ministry.

On Thanksgiving I went to my father's house. Nobody had told me that a relative on his wife's side had just miscarried. When she approached me, I was confused. Seeing her flat belly, I wasn't sure of the timing. Was she not showing yet? Had she already had the baby? I fumbled and said something like, "I hear something big happened to you this year."

She instantly burst into tears and told me of her loss earlier *that week.*

I then received a message that the fetus had been female and I said without thinking, "I'm sorry you lost her."

She replied, "I also had the feeling she was a girl."

We talked a bit about her fear of dying and leaving her other children—which she had shared with me at a previous gathering some months prior, when I first told her about Jean's manifestations. On this night, she told me that my stories had been comforting in that they helped her to know that the spirit lives on, but they were just theoretical. Now, she was experiencing loss firsthand.

I said perhaps she could view this recent loss as a gift from spirit. If she could allow herself to connect with the baby in spirit form, she could not only heal her grief but also heal her terror of dying and leaving her living children, since connecting with her lost baby would give her proof that relationships don't end in death. She cried and told me that she felt grateful and filled with hope.

I invited her to approach me any time during the gathering, if she wanted to talk more about her loss. She voluntarily approached me later, and we talked some more.

A couple of days later (on Jean's birthday, to be exact), I received a call from my father. He told me that this relative had cried for several hours later that night. I was told that she said that I had accosted her while her coat was still on and brought up the subject of her loss. She said that I later forced her to talk, and that she suffered through the discussion to be polite. This was not at all what had transpired!

My father was furious. I was told that I was now uninvited from the upcoming Christmas and New Year's celebrations since that relative would be present and she didn't want to be anywhere near me. I was also told that I would never be allowed to attend family gatherings again.

OVER THE DAYS THAT FOLLOWED, my father interrogated me like a criminal on the witness stand. I was being convicted without a trial. Just like when I was young, I was being beaten down.

I told him that this story was far more complicated than it seemed on the surface. I explained the sequence and tone of events, including that this person had approached me voluntarily and that our conversation was positive. I also shared that crying in such early stages of grief is normal, as is having intense shifts in perspective when talking about the loss. He refused to hear anything I said. He was in a rage. He had to be right, to win. He continued the confrontation over e-mail, never letting up.

I was so tired and beaten down from days and days of his interrogations and assaults. I kept writing to him, trying to get him to see reason. I offered to speak with this relative and do what I could to make amends. But I was told that I would never be permitted to speak to her again.

Finally, I saw my entire childhood pass before my eyes. My father was making me doubt the best part of myself and trashing my newly burgeoning ministry before it was born. Either I was going to lie down and let him kill me, or I was going to stand tall and stand my ground.

I told my father that the details of the case weren't the real point. He was more interested in grinding me into the dirt than having a relationship with me. I told him that I didn't want to walk on eggshells any longer in order to avoid his attacks. I didn't want him belittling me and forcing me to yield to his view and opinions. I asked him to respect me even if he doesn't agree with me. He told me that *he* was sick of walking on eggshells around *me,* and that if I wanted a relationship with him, I'd have to suck it up and take whatever he dished out.

It was then that Jean showed me the road I had to take. I could no longer allow myself to be crushed by my father. Nor could I continue to allow my light to be stamped out in exchange for avoiding verbal humiliation.

Jean was letting me know that my self-esteem could never be whole so long as I continued to interact with someone who beat me down.

I found the courage to tell my father that what he was demanding was a dictatorship, not a relationship, and that if he wanted a relationship he would have to care about how his words and actions landed.

I'm sad to say that he told me, "I am done."

OF COURSE, THE PROSPECT OF BEING ALONE without a father was painful and frightening. I understood why women tolerate abuse. Having a daddy in my life meant that I had a safety net, some insurance against life's dangers. What if I became truly ill? What if I needed help? Despite my fears, despite all the loss I'd suffered recently, despite the fact that I dreaded losing contact with my father, I knew that for my own sake and for the sake of Jean's and my ministry, I had to let go.

Sadly, all this came down the week before Christmas. I felt completely orphaned, since I'd stepped away from my mother during the past year (which I'll discuss more in a bit).

So there I was, alone for Christmas and New Year's, and I was feeling very sad. But Jean's miracles kept on coming.

Chapter 9

Dialoguing to
Bring Me Comfort

After such a painful rift
Let me bring you a special gift

The morning of January 2, Jean's and my wedding anniversary, I was standing in the dining room when I again felt Jean's now familiar tidal wave of love entering me. I heard him tell me that he was sending a man to me. He insisted that I post my profile at a specific site. I'd never intended to engage in Internet dating, and I resisted for days. But Jean kept insisting.

So I finally followed his directions to the specific site, where I began browsing. Out of thousands and thousands of profiles, Jean magnetically pulled me to *one* man's information. At which point, the following thought popped into my head: *I will post my profile (without a photo), and as soon as I do, this man will write to me.* And that's exactly what happened!

As soon as the man and I spoke on the phone, I had the oddest "hit the ground running" feeling. We instantly connected. I felt as if I were speaking with Jean and picking up where we had left off in life.

Because he lived in Florida, there was no way to meet any time soon, so we just spoke by phone.

One night he said, "I see us being very old and dying in each other's arms." He then said that he would "live to be very old and die with me"—Jean's exact words to me when he lived in a body!

In another conversation that was emotional in nature, he paused and said, "I realize that I shouldn't change the level." I nearly dropped the phone. I had taught Jean this lesson, along with the technical term "changing the level," which I discuss in my book *Kiss Your Fights Good-bye*.

In another call, I said, "Don't you want to know what I look like?" (I still hadn't sent my picture.)

He said, "I don't care."

Up to this point, I hadn't told him my last name or that I was known as Dr. Love, so he couldn't have seen a photo of me. But to my astonishment, he described my features: small mouth, straight white teeth, tiny waist, short curly hair (I had short hair at the time). He even mentioned that I smelled like roses— and for months, I had been wearing Jurlique rose hand cream! I was shocked.

In one conversation, I voiced my deepest and most secret concern—that my bodily imperfections, which were the result of having been 300 pounds followed by rapid weight loss, would turn a man off. I told him, "I have physical flaws. I have hanging flesh on my stomach."

He said, "If it's a part of you, it's not a flaw."

I literally wept in relief. This man was telling me what Jean had always said: He loved me no matter what. Jean was letting me know that another man could feel this way about me, too.

At this point, I was sure that Jean had sent me his clone just as he'd promised he would! So, I let down my guard and opened my heart.

It was decided that I would go to Florida and meet this man in six weeks. Long story short, the week I was to go to Florida, he disappeared. It was as if the hand of God had reached down from the heavens and plucked him from my life.

Since I'd already bought my ticket, I figured I would go to Florida all the same. Maybe he would resurface by the time I got there. But when I arrived at the airport, I discovered that my flight—all flights—had been cancelled due to high winds. Then I hit bottom. I was so bereft.

HOW COULD JEAN HAVE DONE THIS to me? Clearly he would never have intentionally hurt me by sending his clone only to yank him from me. So, the only logical conclusion I could come up with was that I had been mistaken from the start. Jean's spirit didn't live on after all.

In my haze of grief, the splinter of a thought kept piercing my consciousness. I sensed that I wasn't properly interpreting what had happened. I recalled the wave of love that preceded my finding this man. I recalled how strongly I felt pushed to him by Jean. My instincts told me that Jean had sent this man to me as a gift of love—and on our anniversary no less.

I began to sense that Jean had chosen to speak through this man at a time when I was so sad over having recently lost my father. It seemed Jean knew that he needed to communicate with me through a living man who could speak his words and offer me a more palpable sense of his presence. Obviously, an animal wouldn't have sufficed!

People kept insisting that I was wrong in my interpretation. Jean would never have chosen to speak to me through *this* guy. He was a con man out to either steal my money or run a head trip on a lonely widow, whom he could emotionally seduce and then drop. Everyone insisted that he was an evil monster.

I began to waver and doubted Jean's presence again. One night, as I wept in despair, I said aloud, "I need a sign of your presence right now. Could you repeat that trick of having my number appear on someone's caller ID? Could you do the trick using Donna [my housekeeper and friend] this time?"

I swear to God, within seconds, Donna phoned and asked, "Did you just call? My phone just rang and your number came up on my caller ID"!

YOU WOULD THINK THAT THIS INSTANT RESPONSE to my plea and the miraculous repeat caller ID phone trick would have convinced me that Jean had, indeed, chosen to convey his presence to me through this man, but in the weeks that followed, my friends' insistence that I was wrong caused me to doubt once more.

I *again* fell into deep sadness. This time, it weakened me, and I developed a severe chest cough. As I lay in bed, almost unable to breathe, I feared that I was going to suffocate the way Jean had.

I again begged Jean for a sign. I said, "If you sent this man as an instrument to speak your words of love to me so that I could feel your presence in my life, and, perhaps, to prove to me that you have the power to send me your real, earthly clone when the time is right, I beg you to please give me a sign *right now* that my interpretation was correct."

Amazingly, after six weeks of silence, the man "rose from the dead" and sent me an e-mail at that very moment! In the message, he asked how I was feeling.

That was all the proof I needed, plain for me to see! Jean had, indeed, sent me this man after my heart had been so broken by my father. He used this man as his mouthpiece, which explained why his words were Jean's, which made it easy for me to have made the mistake of thinking that he was the clone Jean had promised to send me. Jean was proving to me that he simply used the man in the service of love.

Again, on this night, Jean took advantage of this man's openness to move him to write to me, in order to not only answer my request for proof that he had selected a mouthpiece but also prove to me that he is always here with me.

But on this night Jean didn't prop up the man or guide him in what words to say to me. The e-mail I received was awkward. It made no reference to his having ignored my last e-mail and phone call. There was no explanation or apology for having disappeared for six weeks, which permanently turned me off to him.

Had this person been into a con game, he would have been slick and said just what was needed to lure me back into his life. By allowing the man to be himself and reveal his own character flaws, Jean was proving that the man was, indeed, no con artist and that I had read Jean correctly. Jean simply sent this man to love me for a time. But this poor individual was a broken soul with whom I could never have made a life. It was clear that he wasn't the man for me. Had Jean propped him up and given him the right words to say in this final e-mail, I might have been tempted to resume ongoing contact. Instead, Jean simply used him to contact me one final time so that I could understand his purpose. Clearly, Jean wanted me to also know that he ain't the one. Jean showed me that he was just rolling up his sleeves—proving the power he has to send me the right man when the time is right!

THE NEXT MORNING, I READ A PASSAGE in a book that referred to spirits feeling annoyed when they're constantly called upon by the living. Doing so prevents them from pursuing their heavenly work. I worried that I might be impeding Jean in some way . . . but then forgot about it.

Later that night, I was watching a romantic film called *The Sleeping Dictionary*. I suddenly felt Jean's energy all around me. I heard him say, *I am as lost without you as you are without me.*

I was amazed and sad to know that he was as bereft as I was over our being physically separated. His deep yearning to be close to me was palpable. In that moment, I felt him enveloping me in a blanket of love. I felt his ongoing adoration and devotion to me. I again received the message that our destinies were bound together, and that it was his destiny to work with me in our ministry until I return to him. I knew that it would be my challenge to find a way to become comfortable with what we had, rather than continue yearning for what we didn't.

I went to the local zoo the next day. As I entered, I silently asked Jean to speak to me through one of the animals. As I passed through the gate, an emu that was far away came rushing up to the fence where I was standing. He stuck his head through the wire mesh and frantically began wiggling his beak. I saw him move his beak three times, like he was saying, "I love you." Our little pet canary, Fluffy, used to do exactly that! The emu paused a second and did it again. As he wiggled his beak three times, his head was bobbing back and forth. I immediately had the sense that Jean was frantically trying to come through to me.

A couple standing beside me remarked aloud, "Look, that bird seems to be trying to talk to her!" Their observation was all the confirmation I needed.

This experience with the emu proved what I'd heard Jean telling me the night before, that he needed to stay connected to me as much as I needed to stay connected to him. In other words, our inseparability in life continued unchanged. We simply could not be parted.

As I made my way through the zoo, passing from pen to pen, animals stayed next to me, not moving for as long as I wished to stay with them. I was again being reminded that Jean is always by my side. The experience was divine.

A COUPLE OF WEEKS LATER, Ann phoned. She said she was thinking about the man I'd met online and was still convinced that he was a con man.

As I fell asleep, I said to myself, *I must take it as a leap of faith that my interpretation is correct—that Jean's spirit does, indeed, enter bodies (human and animal) in order to connect with me.*

But further proof was what Jean delivered the next morning. His timing was impeccable, as always. On this morning, he moved a woman named Kris, whom I had just met, to call me. She said that when I recently told her the story of Mark and his choking on his way home from my appointments, she was so shocked that she couldn't speak. Now that she had gathered herself, she had to tell me that she, too, had found herself overwhelmed by excess phlegm after each of our visits. She said, "I never would have made the connection to Jean had you not told me the story about what happened to Mark!"

That did it! I finally realized what Jean meant when he said that he would send me his clone. I'd made the mistake of interpreting his words too literally. What he meant was that he would send me his *energetic* clone! In other words, freed from the vessel of his body, he was pure energy. Therefore, his "energetic clone" could be found in every living being. Because I had just lost my father, Jean knew that I needed a living, breathing, and *speaking* human being (as opposed to an animal) to serve as his energetic clone.

As I realized this, I heard Jean say, *Let me love you through whomever I can. Sometimes I love you through a man . . . and sometimes, I love you through an emu!* There he was, rhyming again!

Through this elaborate manifestation that involved many players, both human and animal, Jean was showing me that he can and does love me through whatever instrument he chooses, gracing me and the instrument simultaneously. As Jean moves another person to shower me in his love, that person is being assisted in stretching his or her own spiritual muscles, learning to be more loving of others, which is our most vital spiritual lesson of all.

Meanwhile, Jean told me, *It's time to roll up your sleeves, get back to work, finish this book, and launch our ministry!*

But in order to ready me for the launch of this ministry, Jean needed to bring me one final, cataclysmic healing.

CHAPTER 10

DIALOGUING TO HEAL MY HEART AND SOUL

Now let me make you whole
By healing you heart and soul
For you must truly love yourself
To achieve the pinnacle of spiritual wealth

A year and a half after Jean's departure, the stress of grief had seriously weakened my lungs. I developed pneumonia and was put on strict doses of antibiotics. To my horror, I began ballooning out again.

Discovering one morning that I could no longer fit into my new size-four wardrobe, I became hopelessly upset and collapsed onto the floor of my closet, crying. I was terrified of becoming obese again, but most of all terrified that the priest was right: Jean's miracle was being taken away because Jean was in heaven and gone from my life. Now, I was truly alone.

For a half hour, I wept. This was the day that I so wanted to call my friend Ann and talk to her, but I couldn't bring myself to get up off the floor to dial the phone.

Then, as I described earlier, my phone rang and Ann asked me if I had called her. And when I said no, she told me that obviously Jean had dialed her number and put my information on her caller ID so that she would call me immediately.

I knew that this sign was Jean's way of letting me know that he was with me even in my despair over the weight gain. But I was still deeply tormented. If he gave me the miracle of the weight loss to prove his presence, why take the gift away?

I spent weeks agonizing over this question. I realized that when Jean first left his body, he had to prove his presence in my life beyond the shadow of a doubt. So he brought me the miracle of the weight loss as an emergency form of life support. For me, what greater proof of his presence could he have offered? Clearly the gift wasn't of this world since no earthly means had ever made a dent in the problem. The gift showed me the power of spirit, of Jean, in my life.

In conjunction with this gift, I'd heard him telling me that he was working along with God and the saints to help me. So the weight loss was also his way of bringing God to me, the atheist.

On yet another level, the physical transformation also showed me that miracles are possible when I am one with Jean in spirit. Immediately after he left his body, it was easy for me to be one with him. I was broken wide open. His spirit could enter every crevice of my soul.

So why was the miracle taken from me?

As I reflected, I came to see that on some level, my weight was my educational primer. All my spiritual lessons seemed to be siphoned through this sieve. And, as I was learning, God will put a spiritual lesson before us again and again till we finally get it.

But what was my lesson? In answer to this question, Jean appeared to me in a vision. I saw his graceful hands pulling a long, black snake out of my liver. I had no clue what this vision meant or how it answered my question.

At the same time, my thoughts kept returning to fire. I knew the fire of spirit was key somehow. It was what initially consumed me and burned away my water retention. Was my water weight a sign of spiritual disconnection? If spirit and God are love . . . was I somehow blocking love?

As I reflected further, I had to admit that like so many people who have been abused in childhood, I was capable of giving love, but I was blocked from fully allowing love to enter me.

I knew by this point that Jean had been sent as my intercessor with God—to bring God's love to me. I would never forget the day I left my family to move in with him. The night before leaving home, I had a dream. A large tree gracefully bent its branches in front of my bedroom window. As I climbed out of my window and onto the tree limb, it transformed into a human arm— Jean's arm—that tenderly lowered me to the earth. Then Jean and I drove off together in a bulldozer to face our new life side by side, in which Jean always showered me with unearthly love and guarded me against the assaults of my parents.

So why was it that a lifetime of love from Jean didn't fully penetrate the deepest part of myself? Why hadn't his love exorcised what felt like an internal demon that ravaged me in the form of a self-denigrating voice that put me down and tormented me? Why did I so often feel trapped in a pit with a venomous snake that was relentlessly biting me and poisoning me from within?

This poison was causing horrible reflux. My throat was killing me. I was hoarse. It hurt to talk, and even water burned. I feared I was going to die from this. But I didn't want to take drugs to mask the symptom. I had to get at the cause and resolve it.

ONE DAY, I FELT JEAN LEADING me to his desk drawer. I reached inside and found an angry note that he'd written to himself about me. In it, he expressed his frustration with me. He was so annoyed that he couldn't reach me. No matter how he tried to make me believe how wonderful I was, he said his words never reached the deepest fibers of my soul. No matter how many times he told me how brilliant and accomplished I was, his words were just "tiny drops of water that temporarily quenched [my] thirst" but never filled the empty well inside me. What he meant was that his words didn't fully penetrate my soul because I never fully allowed his love to completely enter me.

I was horrified to find this letter. I was ashamed of his depiction of me. My friend Ann was sure that I was never meant to find it. She said that he had written it to vent his spleen on a day when he was angry with me, and he'd obviously shoved the letter in the drawer and forgotten about it. She asked me to burn it. I did burn the letter, but I couldn't shake the feeling that he had meant for me to find it; there was something he wanted me to learn about myself, a lesson he wanted to impart. I knew the answer was close, like the forgotten idea that slips from the cliff of consciousness, the lost word that tickles the tip of your tongue. From that day forward, the question festered within my soul like an embedded splinter. I had to know what he wanted me to learn about myself.

To answer this, I knew I had to dig into my earliest memories.

As I SAID PREVIOUSLY, I WAS BORN three months early while my parents were spending the weekend visiting friends who lived in Boston. I weighed only two pounds and was left in the hospital for the first three months of my life. My parents returned to New Jersey after I was born. I still don't know why my mother didn't stay with me, since she wasn't working and she could have. She told me years later that she called me on the phone each day.

When I finally came home from the hospital, I cried constantly, my mother later told me. I was so depressed that I dragged my chin along the floor, unable to lift my head. She never picked me up or hugged me in affection, never snuggled in bed with me, never held me in her arms or on her lap. In fact, in my baby photos I was always alone. Later, whenever I tried to touch her, she pushed me away.

In addition to fear of abandonment, all my childhood memories are a collage of verbal and physical beatings from both my mother and father. I never felt loved or lovable. Put-downs formed the fabric—more like the crazy quilt—of my self-image.

I recalled a day when I was a toddler and my mother came after me, brandishing a hairbrush, screaming like she was on the warpath. She beat my bare bottom with those stiff black bristles to retaliate against me for whatever horrible offense I had committed. Even as a young child, I sensed that my offense was being born.

As soon as we heard my father's key in the lock, she would run alongside me to get to my father first. Like a sibling, not a mother, she wanted him to hear her side of the story before I could tell him how I'd been mistreated. The goal was to get him to side with her against me, to induce him to punish or beat me. This act of loyalty would temporarily cement their bond, as I said previously.

Whenever I balked over her attacks, she would turn the tables. She'd deny having said what I just heard her say (which made me feel insane) and she'd accuse me of being paranoid and crazy. At the same time, she'd tell me that I didn't love her. If I did, I wouldn't think she was being critical. She would accuse me of abusing and victimizing her by misinterpreting her words. She would then withdraw from me, saying that she needed to lick her wounds. She'd give me the silent treatment for weeks and refuse to feed me so that I had to pull a chair up to the stove and cook for myself. This silent treatment would continue until I apologized. Because I needed my mommy, I always did come back and say I was sorry.

From the earliest age, however, I knew that I was the one who had been abused, not the other way around. I learned later that "gas-lighting" (a tactic in which a person's reality is called into doubt) is a prime cause of insanity.

I also realized early on that, similar to my father, my mother was reliving her own childhood trauma through me. She patterned herself after her own mother who said and did mean, hurtful things. Because she was treated this way, she gave herself license to say whatever came into her head.

DURING GRAD SCHOOL (WHICH MY parents promised to pay for but then refused to) I took classes at night, worked until 3 A.M. as a cocktail waitress, and went to field placement during the day. One day, during the fall semester, my mother picked a fight with me, accusing me of having put a dirty dish in the already clean dishwasher. I hadn't. She flew into a rage. She pushed me out the door and locked it. She shouted, "You don't have a mother anymore!"

I drove to Jean's apartment in a state of terrible distress. I was obviously being reminded on a cellular level of my early birth and the first three months of my life when I'd been left in the hospital. It was following this argument that my mother instructed my father to write to me and cut me off financially. This was the start of my uncontrollable water retention and weight gain.

Jean was in Europe at the time, but I had a key to his apartment. When Jean returned, we met with my parents at a restaurant in New Jersey. He asked them to honor their promise to fund my graduate school studies, but they refused. My mother began berating me, enumerating my various sins and failures. I remember suddenly feeling what it must be like to go mad. I was no longer in my body. I was under water. Her words were garbled, and I couldn't hear anymore.

Jean and I left the restaurant and returned to his apartment in Poughkeepsie. I obtained a scholarship and worked as the assistant to the dean. With Jean's help, I managed to complete my graduate studies.

My parents divorced around this time, and I went on to become a therapist.

JEAN AND I SAW MY NOW-DIVORCED parents throughout our nearly three-decade marriage. Thankfully, Jean's watchful eyes had the effect of holding their behavior somewhat in check.

But when Jean died of the bee sting, my earthly bodyguard was gone, as I said, and I was thrown once more into the pit of snakes. Once I was alone and vulnerable, my mother had resumed biting me without restraint.

One day while visiting me soon after Jean's death, she saw a picture of me taken at the time when I first met Jean. She said, "If you looked like that now you'd find another man. You'll never meet anyone looking the way you do."

I so often felt defective and mutilated by her words. They cut more deeply than a surgeon's knife. I was starting to see why in my own self-talk I tore myself to shreds. I was mimicking the master.

By a year or so after Jean's death, I had stepped away from my mother following one of her particularly awful verbal beatings. Then, after my father walked away from me, I resumed contact with her. As a new widow, the last thing I wanted was to be without a mother, too. But in no time, she began playing upon my weakness by telling me more monstrous things than ever before.

I was starting to see that whenever I was weak, she would abuse me because she couldn't tolerate weakness in anyone. Yet whenever I felt strong, she'd tear me down out of jealousy.

On some level, I knew that all this mistreatment was an essential part of my destiny. It impelled me to create the Dr. Love ministry, with its central focus to guide people to be loving and respectful even when they're feeling angry. Clearly, the abuse I suffered drove me to inspire people to treat one another kindly and fight to make the world a better place.

EVEN THOUGH I KNEW THERE WAS a reason for all of this, I still needed to find a way to save myself. My mother's mean words continued to buzz in my head like a swarm of killer bees, destroying my confidence and peace. As long as my mother's voice lived inside me, I knew that I would suffer. This was my time of gestation and rebirth. I had to be delivered of her toxic, critical voice because it tore me down and drowned out Jean's words of love. The more she ravaged and tortured me, the less I could hear Jean, and the more alone and terrified I felt. I didn't know what to do.

On the morning of my birthday, Jean came to me in a dream with a clear warning. He stood behind me, his arms wrapped around me, protecting me while I faced my mother.

He was showing me that he "had my back" as I faced the attack that was coming. Since he'd never done anything like this before, I knew that he was making sure that I paid attention. In the dream, Jean told me that she was the snake that he was pulling from my body, the venom that was inside me, the voice that ravaged me, the poison in my liver, the burning in my guts.

I was amazed that Jean knew she was going to be taking me out that night. On my birthday, he was clearly working to complete my healing and rebirth.

AT DINNER WITH MY MOTHER that evening, I confided that I was nervous about an upcoming medical procedure—an endoscopy. I'd undergone this test once before and was terribly violated. The doctor had promised that Jean could stay with me. But when the test began, the doctor told Jean to leave. He refused, saying that he promised he'd stay. The doctor, in a fit of rage, rammed the endoscopy tube down my throat, choking me while I was still awake. It was a nightmare to be strapped down and subjected to this kind of abuse, and I was terrified at the prospect of being subjected to such an ordeal again—and on my own this time.

"I don't know what's wrong with you. I've never met anyone who chooses such bad doctors," she said irritably.

I felt slapped in the face. I said, "You're telling me I'm an idiot. This doctor was highly recommended. How would I have known that he would act that way when he was angry?" I tried to talk to her and tell her that I felt hurt, but my words were gas thrown on a fire.

She turned the tables and issued her familiar refrain: I was abusing her. She said I always assigned the worst meaning to her words, which proved I didn't love her.

"Instead of hearing me, you're counter-blaming," I explained.

"How's this for counter-blaming? Go fuck yourself."

I was incensed. "How can you accuse me of abusing you, when you just told me to go fuck myself? You should be ashamed," I said in an even tone.

She bolted from the restaurant, and I got stuck with the check. By this point, I was practically foaming at the mouth. I forced myself to contain my anger. On the drive home in my car, she berated me. There it was: My entire lifetime with her was passing in front of my eyes, culminating in this current fireworks finale of attacks.

"I've been calm with you this entire time, despite the fact that I'm very angry," I said. "The problem is that whenever I try to say how I feel about something that was said or done, you feel insulted and attacked and then you turn the tables back on me. And then I'm never heard."

But she kept shooting one poisonous verbal dart after another.

When we reached my house, she gave me a sad, despondent look. As she got into her car and backed out, I knew that I would never hear from her again if I didn't reach out to her. But I resisted doing what I'd always done in the past. I wasn't going to suck up and play nice. No more rewarding her abuse.

Even though I had no more contact with my mother, I was disappointed to discover that my mind wasn't quiet. Her put-downs still rang in my head. And as I continued to listen to my nasty self-talk, I realized that much of my self-loathing was directed at my body. I loved myself thin and hated myself when I was fat.

As I reflected on my miraculous weight loss, I realized that Jean initially brought me that miracle to prove his presence. But clearly, the weight loss had to be reversed to expose my lack of true self-love. I recalled a novel in which a dog was used to assist a healer. He could sniff out abscesses that lay deep beneath the skin. As I was realizing, my self-loathing was an abscess that was hidden by the false self-love that I felt when I was thin.

I knew that the most important spiritual question of my life was being put to me: Would I not only accept and surrender to being heavy, but also love myself at any size? I again recalled the frustrated letter I found in Jean's drawer, in which he railed on about my unwillingness to absorb his love for me. Jean adored me fat or thin. Paradoxically, I was being asked to *earn* his miraculous gift of weight loss by being willing to give it up and love myself even if I wasn't thin.

In that moment, Jean brought me his ultimate gift of healing. I suddenly saw him appear before me. He was surrounded in golden light. He tenderly held my face in his hands and turned me toward the light.

Then I heard him say in a soft, gentle tone, *Listen, listen, listen.* He meant for me to turn my focus from my toxic parents' voices and *listen* to his voice and words of love.

He put his hands over my ears and kissed my lips, silencing me. Then he said, *Hear no evil. Speak no evil.*

In that moment, I knew why all the decades of therapy hadn't enabled me to rid myself of my parents' poisonous words. The official therapy party line was that the voice of the therapist should replace the parent's voice. My professional group had told me, "Just hear us shouting at your parents and drowning them out." But they could never outyell my parents' voices.

If I would simply allow Jean's loving voice to enter me, however, it would drown them out. And again, I thought about Jean's frustrated letter. I still needed to know why I hadn't fully absorbed his love when he lived in a body.

The answer came as I began to feel Jean begging to enter me completely, begging me to allow him to fill me so there would be no space within my vessel for any toxic influences. He told me that there would be no room for him as long as my parents' poison filled me. To be born again, I had to allow his love to fully enter me, to purge myself of their poison.

At the same moment, I realized that the water that my body held was a re-creation of the water that surrounds and protects us in the womb. Even though Jean protected me in his earthly form, there was a limit in his ability to reach me.

MY ENTIRE STORY BECAME CLEAR. Jean had to be in spirit form in order for me to complete my healing! He had to be freed from the vessel of his own physical body in order for his unearthly love for me, along with his soul essence, to enter me unimpeded.

An overwhelming feeling of love filled me—it was Jean, of course. As he entered me fully, I had no choice but to love myself as he did. And at last, I *fully* understood what Jean meant when he promised to send me his clone. At first, he brought me his spirit in the form of animals and humans who were open enough to speak his words of love. Ultimately, he implanted the clone of his spirit within me: His love was my self-love! In other words, the clone of his soul essence had entered me and woven itself into the fabric of my DNA. Jean's energetic clone was within me!

Finally, I was blinded from seeing or feeling anything but his love and light. For the first time in my life, I couldn't help but love myself completely. I'd had to wait until he was no longer in bodily form for his ultimate gift to me to be fulfilled—for his love for me to become my self-love.

From that moment on, his words have continued to ring out like glorious church bells singing our never-ending love song.

OUR SONG IS YOURS, TOO, for your loved ones in spirit are also sending themselves to you. Eventually, as you open yourself to a direct dialogue, you, too, will feel the love of their spirits within you, assisting you in putting to rest any outstanding relationship issues that may be lingering and helping you to heal yourself, body, mind, and soul.

So without further ado, let's remove any obstacles to your connecting with loved ones in spirit, so that they may shower you in love and heal every corner of your being and life.

PART II

Dispelling Harmful Beliefs

CHAPTER 11

REMOVING OBSTACLES TO SPIRIT COMMUNICATION

You can allow the mystery to unfold
By not believing everything you've been told

In this chapter, I'll share some fundamental concepts that prove why connecting with the spirit of our loved ones is an innate, albeit often uncultivated, ability. My purpose is to banish any lingering doubts, prejudices, or biases that may hinder your own process of reconnection.

I know that what I report flies in the face of logic and natural laws. A research scientist once told me that when he conducts experiments, if a finding occurs a single time, it may be attributed to coincidence or chance; but when the same outcome occurs three separate times, it's considered a scientifically valid result. As you will see, each type of manifestation that Jean has offered has been repeated not three times, but more than 3,000 times.

Prominent Support for Spirit Communication

After I wrote this book, I discovered that many prominent figures throughout history, from Socrates to Helen Keller, have reported having personal contact with spirits.

Sigmund Freud wrote in 1921, "If I had my life to live over again, I should devote myself to psychical research rather than to psychoanalysis." Carl Jung, Swiss psychotherapist and the founder of analytical psychology, also wrote extensively on this subject.

Thomas Edison said in an interview in *Scientific American,* "It's reasonable to conclude that those who have left this earth would like to communicate with those they have left here." And "I do claim that it is possible to construct an apparatus which will be so delicate that if there are personalities in another existence or sphere who wish to get in touch with us . . . this apparatus will at least give them a better opportunity." He was working on such an apparatus when he died in 1931. Even the great scientist Albert Einstein, in his introduction to Upton Sinclair's book on telepathy, *Mental Radio,* called on science to take such phenomena seriously.

For decades scientific research has been uncovering evidence that human consciousness (or what some call the soul) lives on after bodily death.

Max Planck, who received the 1918 Nobel Prize and is recognized as the father of quantum physics, said in The Observer (January 25, 1931) that his experiments indicated that human consciousness pre-existed the universe. As he said, "I regard consciousness as fundamental. I regard matter as derivative from consciousness. We cannot get behind consciousness. Everything that we talk about, everything that we regard as existing, postulates consciousness."

David Bohm, a protégé of Einstein and one of the world's most respected quantum physicists, was himself a proponent of the holographic model precisely because it explains various phenomena for which both traditional and quantum physics have no explanation.

Stuart Hameroff, Ph.D., and Deepak Chopra, M.D., recently published an article entitled "The Quantum Soul: A Scientific Hypothesis," in which they say, "End-of-life brain activity supports the notion of a quantum basis for consciousness which could conceivably exist independent of biology in various scalar planes in spacetime geometry."

According to Michael Talbot, author of the *The Holographic Universe*, "Some scientists are beginning to believe the universe itself is a kind of giant hologram, a splendidly detailed illusion." Talbot goes on to say that the holographic model explains all paranormal and mystical experiences, from telepathy, precognition, and mystical feelings of oneness with the universe, to psychokinesis, which is the ability of the mind to move physical objects without anyone touching them. It even explains death itself, which is nothing more than the shifting of a person's consciousness from one level of the hologram of reality to another.

The brilliant Thomas Campbell has spent the past 30 years studying the properties, boundaries, and abilities of consciousness. In his seminal work *My Big TOE,* Campbell presents his consciousness theory of everything, including what he calls a virtual reality concept, which explains how multiple realities exist simultaneously. His larger consciousness system (LCS) explains all paranormal or psi experiences, including the placebo effect, quantum entanglement, precognition, out-of-body experience (OOBE), near-death experience (NDE), after-death communication (ADC), and even aspects of dreaming, particularly lucid dreaming.

A fascinating article at www.spiritscienceandmetaphysics.com entitled "Scientists Claim That Quantum Theory Proves Consciousness Moves to Another Universe at Death" says that we carry space and time around with us "like turtles with shells." According to Dr. Robert Lanza, who was voted the third-most-important scientist alive by *The New York Times,* when the shell comes off (space and time), we still exist.

In his book, Lanza argues that the death of consciousness simply does not exist. He explains that humans wrongly assume that the body generates consciousness, and that consciousness dies with the body. But according to Lanza, we receive consciousness in the same way that a cable box receives satellite signals. The signals do not end with death, which means consciousness is not constrained by time, space, the body, or the brain. As Lanza says, consciousness is nonlocal in the same way that quantum objects are nonlocal.

Prominent afterlife researcher Roberta Grimes has gathered much of the evidence for the survival of consciousness in her wonderfully accessible book *The Fun of Dying.* She says, "Evidence tells us that there are about seven inhabited levels of after-death reality that are separated from us and from each other only by their differing energy levels, just as television channels exist at different vibratory rates." She adds, "The evidence overwhelmingly indicates that when we die, we simply tune our minds away from this material channel to one at a slightly higher rate of vibration, and there we pick up a whole new solid post-death reality."

Grimes further argues that the more than 95 percent of the universe that physicists identify as "dark matter" and "dark energy" because it won't interact with material light looks suspiciously like the greater reality that we enter at death. Scientists have no better explanation for it. So perhaps mainstream scientists have discovered the afterlife after all!

Grimes also states that the Human Genome Project decisively puts to bed the possibility that our brains generate our minds. It was revealed in 2014 that the human genome contains only 19,000 genes, which is 2,000 fewer than the genome of *C. elegans,* a nearly microscopic worm of fewer than a thousand cells. And nearly all of our genes predate the emergence of primates. As Grimes says, "The implications of the fact that the human genome is so small have not been well publicized, but many researchers are stunned by it. Either much of what they thought about genetics is wrong, or the human brain does not generate the mind."

Grimes argues that the evidence is overwhelming that our minds are powerful parts of an energy-like consciousness matrix. Her research agrees with the work of the founding quantum physicists in demonstrating that human consciousness is primary and preexisting. It easily survives the death of our bodies.

Dean Radin, author of *The Conscious Universe,* eloquently concludes, "I've . . . learned that those who loudly assert with great confidence that there isn't any scientifically valid evidence for psychic abilities don't know what they're talking about."

Sadly, most of us are unaware that such great scientific minds believe not only that beings live on in spirit form, but also that they can continue to communicate with us.

What's worse, after Jean left his body in 2006, I discovered that many Christians are riddled with false teachings and beliefs that block their ability to communicate with spirit beings. On more than one occasion since Jean left his body, priests have told me that the spirit lingers close to the earth for only a short while after death, and that once our loved ones are in heaven they are forever out of reach, incommunicado. Any attempt to make contact with the spirit world at this point is, according to some religious leaders, akin to doing the devil's work. If we accept that paradigm, we're condemned to tolerate an emotional wasteland in which our relationships are held in suspension (and suspense) until we're reunited in death.

Heaven Revealed

Why are we told that we can't communicate with loved ones in heaven? Are there no cell towers there? Are the signals from heaven too weak to reach the earth? It's ludicrous to apply earthly concepts to this alternative realm we call the afterlife or heaven.

Jean wants it known that what we've been told about the after-life is dead wrong, no pun intended. In fact, soon after his death, Jean implanted the following message in my mind: *Heaven is a state, not a place.* The point being, we don't need to wait until we die to be reunited with loved ones in heaven. Heaven is here and now. Heaven is all around us. Heaven is among us.

If you recall, Jean said, *Death is an illusion. There is a very thin veil between the realm where you are and the realm where I am. The veil is thinner than you can ever imagine. I'm standing right here.*

You may also remember that Jean implored me, *Don't leave me, Jamie.* It was at that precise moment that I realized that our loved ones don't abandon us. We leave them!

Why do we do this? It's because, as I stated previously, the human experience is governed by expectations. For example, studies show that if you're told that a medical procedure will be painful, your body will produce a neuropeptide called Substance P, a chemical that is responsible for causing pain in the body. In other words, the anticipation of pain actually produces pain. Likewise, if you're told that you won't hear from loved ones who have passed, you'll shut your ears and close your eyes, and lo and behold, your expectations will be fulfilled. The sad result of such teachings is that they prevent you from realizing that your loved ones are reaching out to you all the time, patiently waiting for you to open the doors of your heart and mind.

If you recall, as I lay alone in Jean's and my bed my first night back from Italy, Jean told me, *I had to go. I needed to be in the form I'm in to help you better.* The next day, when I met with his priest, whom I did not know at all, to prepare the readings for his funeral, I told him what Jean had said to me the previous night.

As I described, when the priest heard what Jean had told me, he blanched and said, "Dear God. At first I didn't believe that Jean was speaking to you. But now I do."

I learned that I was quoting the dying words of St. Dominic, found in the section of the catechism regarding the Communion of Saints. But, as I said, at the time I had never had religious instruction or gone to church—nor had Jean discussed religion with me when he lived in his body—so I obviously had no idea that I was quoting holy words. As time went on, I returned to the rectory to discuss with the priest my continuing experiences with Jean. I was shocked to find the door practically slammed in my face. A devout Catholic friend told me that this priest's reaction was not atypical.

At first I was crushed. Then I began asking why the church doesn't want us to have ongoing communication with those we care about. As I reflected on this question, I had the impression that the church is afraid that the devil can masquerade as our deceased loved ones. I sensed that I was confronting a primitive fear of devil worship or spirit possession—how medieval, how Dark Ages.

When I spoke to a liberal priest who confirmed my suspicions, I came to understand the official party line: In the eyes of the church, it's okay to speak to God and the saints, but the list of whom you may communicate with in the spirit realm ends there.

A year after Jean quoted the words of St. Dominic, I reflected on why he chose to quote this and only this passage, and I finally understood. He was a religious pioneer in life and continues to be one in the afterlife. Those words supporting the doctrine of the Communion of Saints explain that our deceased loved ones are in communion with—are at one with—God and the saints and all other spirit beings and angels, depending upon our orientation.

Jean quoted this passage to confirm an essential truth. Because we're expected to love and engage in ongoing communication with God and the saints, and because our deceased loved ones are at one with God and the saints, we are therefore meant to continue loving and communicating with our loved ones who have passed over.

To drive the point home that he is in communion with God and the saints, Jean has repeatedly said to me, *We are helping you with this . . .* and *Let us take care of that . . .*

When I first heard him speaking this way, I jokingly responded, "Who's this *we*, white man?" It took me quite some time to realize that he was using plural pronouns because he wanted me to understand that he is working in conjunction with God and other spirit beings on my behalf—and therefore on behalf of everyone.

Vessels Through Which Spirit Speaks

During my last visit with Jean's priest—the visit before the door was closed on me—I told him that Jean often speaks to me through others. The priest said that he didn't believe it. But this is not a matter to believe or not. It simply is. Since his death, Jean has offered me numerous examples that all living beings are meant to be God's messengers. They are our intercessors to God. Being open to the concept that our loved ones speak through Open Vessels is essential in removing obstacles to spirit communication.

Traditional Christianity rebuffs the pantheistic idea that humans and animals can be vessels through which a spirit speaks. In researching why this is, I discovered that Genesis 1:1–30 teaches that God is separate from creation. By contrast, pantheism holds that every aspect of creation expresses God's nature and essence.

Because my eyes had not been blinded by official church teachings, I was able to see that God speaks to us through every living being. It therefore makes complete sense that our deceased loved ones (who are one with God) can also speak to us through those who live. Jean has offered me repeated proof that we are meant to receive God's love and that of our deceased loved ones through the people and animals that walk the earth.

We Evolve Through Death

Jean has also shown me that beings evolve when they enter the spirit realm. In spirit form, we become more knowing, more sensing, more seeing. For example, one day soon after Jean left his body, I had to take my car in for service. This is a task that Jean always did, so I didn't know anyone at the garage. As I began talking to Debbie, the woman behind the counter, she told me that she was a widow. That's all she had to say. In seconds, her deceased husband was delivering a message to her through me.

This was the first message that I received from someone other than Jean. I couldn't ignore the sense that the husband was "banging down the door" in order to get through to his wife. He said, "Tell her that she's making the same mistake with our son that I did."

When I told Debbie what her husband had said to me, she blinked in astonishment. The man went on to say that it was his own stubbornness that created the rebellious attitude in their son. She was falling into the same trap, and she must do everything possible to avoid it. Debbie then confirmed the accuracy of this message. So you see, her husband, in spirit form, had received a wake-up call. He knew what he hadn't understood when he lived in his physical body.

It's Never Too Late to Make Peace with the Deceased

As a result of such experiences, I learned that it becomes possible for us to resolve issues that never could have been resolved when our loved ones lived in a body. What's more, it has been revealed to me that the departed yearn to right their wrongs and make amends with the living. This means that it's never too late to heal wounds, resolve resentments, make peace, and restore a damaged relationship. At the same time, please know that if you're carrying resentment toward someone who mistreated or abused you, you're not expected to force forgiveness on yourself. Beings in spirit form accept you as you are, right where you are. You can be angry; you can rage at them for as long as you need to. They aren't going anywhere. They have an eternity to work it out with you! All you need to do is open your heart and allow the process of healing to begin. Allow them to make peace with you and to shower you with love.

~~~~~~

CHAPTER 12

HOW IS SPIRIT COMMUNICATION POSSIBLE?

~~~~~~

Open your eyes and you will see
The constant presence of eternity

As a final preparation for establishing your own communication with spirit, I would first like to discuss why I believe communication with spirit beings is even possible. I must preface this discussion by reminding you that I have no formal religious training. As I've stated previously, I was raised not to believe in God and the afterlife. I never read the Bible, and Jean and I didn't discuss religion, at least while he was alive in physical form. He realized, of course, that I was an atheist, and it was not his nature to try to impose his beliefs on me.

I now understand why we never needed to discuss religion and why we had no difficulty reconciling his faith with my atheism. The reason is because we both lived in the spirit realm most of the time. In living heaven, which is synonymous with love, there was no need to discuss religious theory or doctrine. The one problem we did experience was the result of our returning to earth, if you will. What got in our way was the periodic realization that we would be separated by Jean's impending bodily death. This triggered fear and all the defensive operations that Jean used to hold me off in order to protect me from that loss.

I've also come to realize that Jean and I had an unspoken soul pact that he would establish a ministry through me after his death. And on some level, we both consented to make the sacrifice to be separated in body so that he could fortify my powers as a healer and transmit wisdom from the other side.

In addition, I believe that we were brought together because my well-established ability to communicate energetically (which I'll talk about more later in this chapter) would enable him to speak to me from the beyond, thereby allowing me to transmit his messages to the world. This explains why Jean valued my religious purity. Apart from his respect for my atheism, I think he also didn't bring me to church because he didn't want me to become tainted by official doctrine. He wanted me to remain the open book that I am so that I could receive his messages and not dismiss them as being contrary to accepted wisdom.

I should add that other than *The Secret,* I had never read New Age spiritual writings either. Because I wasn't familiar with these types of works, I was even more open to receive Jean.

It was only after I completed writing this book that I began researching the "competition"—if you can call it that, since books in a certain genre often serve to complement one another rather than compete against one another. I was surprised to discover numerous works by mainstream authors who had written about the afterlife, spirit visitations, soul travel, and so on. As a result of this research, I became familiar with the standard terminology other authors use. Since I didn't learn this until afterward, however, my text does not contain such informed terms. Before Jean's death, I never believed that beings live on in spirit form. It therefore never occurred to me that communication with a loved one's spirit was possible, even though, as I mentioned, I had extensive experience with energetic communication, which I will describe in greater detail in this chapter.

Whether Jean was conscious of this plan before he left his body, I can't say. He didn't articulate his intentions until after his death.

Factors Contributing to Spirit Communication

I have often wondered why this miracle between Jean and me is occurring. I believe our remarkably open channel of communication is the result of the convergence of several factors.

First and foremost is that prior to Jean's death, I was an atheist. In order to prove to me that there is indeed an afterlife, he had to break all the rules and pull out all the stops to make his presence known, leaving no room for doubt. You may wonder why he didn't feel the need to discuss religion and the afterlife with me prior to leaving his body. The answer is straightforward: Jean knew that the best way for me to discover the truth was through firsthand experience. Think of the analogy of an orgasm. Someone can try to describe what an orgasm feels like, but words will never suffice. You just need to feel the sensations for yourself. Likewise, whatever words he might have used to describe spirituality and the afterlife would have paled in comparison. On some level, he just knew that the best way to teach me was to come through in spirit form. His first purpose was to let me know that he continues to love me and watch over me. But, his enduring gift to me becomes a gift to all. Whether or not you currently believe in the spirit world, his gift remains for you to receive.

Certainly our intense love and extremely close connection to each other while Jean lived in a body was a preparation for our spiritual communion after his death. As an aside, before Jean's departure, he often gave me greeting cards that depicted us together as lovers in other eras. At the time, I just thought he was being romantic. Then, after he left his body, he made it clear to me that we actually have always been together. Here's how he explained it to me: All of us begin in spirit form. We have a short ride in a body, and then we return to spirit form again. From what he's shown me, reincarnation doesn't exist as our human minds envision it. It's hard to explain, but he's shown me that past, present, and future don't happen in a continuum. It's more like they're occurring simultaneously. In other words, Jean and I have always been together. For most of our "lives" we have been together in spirit form. We had a short time together in physical form, and now we are together in parallel universes—with me on the earth plane and him in the spirit plane.

He's also explained to me that souls travel in packs or tribes. This may account for why we sometimes feel an instant connection with another person—because we're recognizing a soul that we've already been with in spirit form.

My receptivity is clearly a factor, and last but not least a key ingredient in the mix is Jean's deep spirituality, which remained unchanged despite his having left the priesthood. Jean was, simply put, one with God. Even the Dalai Lama referred to Jean as one of the 50 most spiritual people ever to have lived.

As director of the Center for Emotional Communication, and of course as Dr. Love, I've spent my entire professional career helping people improve relationships. Now more than ever I understand how important it is to perfect our ability to be open to one another and to love one another.

The Importance of Living in the Now

We've all heard how vital it is to live in the present, as opposed to dwelling on what has happened or worrying about what may happen. It is said that this is the key to personal peace and the end of human suffering. To achieve this goal, people strive—often through meditation—to develop an acute sense of awareness of the world around them, thereby allowing them to be more fully present in the now. But this solitary act largely misses the point. I firmly believe that we're supposed to live in the now so that we may be fully present to connect with *others*. Loving others fully is the ultimate in-the-now experience. When we care about people and act on that love in ways that are kind and supportive, we are fulfilling our divine purpose on earth.

Unfortunately, living in the now is easier said than done. Most of us carry what I call Old Scars from childhood. These unhealed wounds create a form of psychological haunting that makes us afraid that nightmares from our past will invade our future. As we limp through life, dragging these phantoms into our every interaction and relationship, our fears are often fulfilled simply because they're *there*.

In order to love fully in the present, we must be liberated from our Old Scars. This is why I have devoted my professional life to helping people identify and heal these early wounds that prevent us from completely loving ourselves, which is the precondition for loving others.

In my book *Kiss Your Fights Good-bye,* I explain that unhealed childhood wounds, or Old Scars, are the underlying cause of *all* relationship conflict. Why? The brain works by association, constantly comparing present events with past experiences. I call this the Emotional Lake Effect. Think about the actual lake effect, in which a storm gathers strength as it picks up moisture crossing the Great Lakes or another large body of water. Our psyches do the same thing. When a present-day incident is reminiscent of an earlier injury, our minds dip into the reservoir of our unconscious and stir up memories of past offenses. The link is made without our consciously knowing it. In no time, fireworks are going off inside of us; we become upset and want to strike out at someone or something but we can't explain why. That's because the entire process is unfolding unconsciously. Intense feelings that we can't seem to shake are the clue that a childhood wound has been awakened. Because early wounds can trigger intense rage, it is easy for us to fall into the fight cycles that destroy love.

At the same time, intimate relationships offer a divine opportunity to help us work together to heal these Old Scars. The key to maintaining loving relationships is to resist the urge to gratify ourselves by saying or doing hurtful or damaging things to another person when we're being buffeted by the Emotional Lake Effect. Instead, we must vow to resist the urge to "get our rocks off" at another person's expense—otherwise our relationships will end up on the rocks! What we must say or do at times such as these is whatever will be helpful to the other person *and* to the relationship. After all, when we do harm to someone else, we ultimately are doing harm to ourselves.

The path to healing ourselves, our relationships, and the world around us is to transform raw angry feelings into communications that are constructive, loving, and healing. As we resist dumping raw emotional sewage on others, as we perfect our ability to listen and understand in the way our parents rarely did for us (for me, anyway), we are helping one another heal these Old Scars. As the wounds heal, anger and fighting and "dis-ease" fade away, allowing love to shine through and disperse the emotional dark clouds.

Obviously, the better you nurture your relationships on earth, the stronger your bonds will be and the easier it will be for you to later connect with your loved ones. Handling anger properly, healing your Old Scars, and dissolving all the walls that block you from loving fully will set the stage for reconnecting with loved ones after they pass. Love is what I call the Currency of Connection. It is what links us with spirit beings.

But don't despair. Even if you didn't have a strong connection with your partner, friend, or relative when he or she lived on earth, it's never too late to connect. Not only will I show you how to renew a relationship with someone who has passed; I will also show you how to make your relationship even better than it was before.

Spiritual Receptivity and Premature Birth

I believe that my being born three months before my due date has contributed to my being exceptionally open to receiving nonverbal energetic communication from animals, people, and spirits without being blocked by the barriers or walls that most individuals build up to protect them from emotional pain. In the psychoanalytic world, there's an established link between premature birth and a lack of psychic insulation. Specifically, Dr. Louis

R. Ormont, the founder of modern group psychoanalysis, super-vised me for two decades. Dr. Hyman Spotnitz, who had been su-pervised by Sigmund Freud, in turn supervised Lou. Dr. Ormont wrote about the concept of an insulation barrier to describe the defensive psychic structure that allows a person to withstand toxic stimuli while enabling nutrient experiences—a psychoana-lytic term meaning any contact that is positive and life affirm-ing—to flow through. Lou told me one day that he was certain my early birth had left me constitutionally uninsulated. For these and related reasons, from a young age I've been able to quickly sense what is ailing people both emotionally and physically.

As a result of my early birth, I also suffered an undetected congenital defect of my urethra. It was so malformed that it was almost sealed shut, which caused urine to back up into the bladder and become infected. These "silent" and undetected infections, in turn, caused me to run deliriously high, 105-degree fevers throughout my childhood.

I believe these fevers drastically altered my brain functions. While Jean still lived in his body, we had already discovered that I have the ability to tune in to various frequencies, which enables me to energetically communicate with and heal wild and domes-tic animals. I also have the ability to tune in to people's bodies and psyches, discern what troubles them, and then heal them ei-ther by a laying on of hands or doing distance healings. What we didn't know at the time was that these fevers also enabled my brain to straddle both this world and the spirit realm, which would soon enable me to openly communicate with that plane.

While writing this book, I discovered that the world-renowned psychic medium George Anderson also suffered an intense fever as a child. When he recovered, his mediumistic ability was well established. Scientists think it's possible that high fever may alter brain function and that this may be a possible explanation for George's (as well as my own) psychic abilities.

In addition, I also discovered that George has an abnormal skull formation. Medical science has hypothesized that this mal-formation could be partly responsible for his abilities. I also have a very pronounced skull indentation (concealed by my hair), which was attributed to my early birth.

I understand that this may all sound extreme, but don't worry! Even if you haven't suffered high fevers and don't have an abnormally shaped skull, you can still develop communication with spirit. In fact, we're all born with these innate abilities, but our upbringing and religious indoctrination forces us to forget what we know.

Awareness and Spirituality

One of the ways of reawakening to these abilities is to fine-tune your openness by consciously being aware of your feelings, another aspect of living in the now. Heightened consciousness is, in fact, the key goal to which all enlightened beings must aspire.

I believe my openness facilitates Jean's ability to reach me. The same reciprocity that exists in earthly relationships exists for spiritual connections. My receptivity to Jean allows him to come to me now. Again, I want to reassure you that even if you aren't currently as open as you'd like to be, as with every other skill, practice makes perfect. I will show you how to cultivate emotional receptivity so that you, too, will soon be capable of sending and receiving communications to and from your loved ones in the spirit realm.

I must also add that spirit communication requires awareness. I used to take my acute awareness for granted, but now I see that it is an essential prerequisite for spirit communication. Most people sleepwalk through their days, unaware of what's going on around them—in effect living with their eyes closed. In order to see the signs of spirit presence that surround us, we must be fully aware. This may sound like a daunting task, but believe me, it *can* be done. Again, practice makes perfect.

People have often said to me, "Don't you think your experiences are unique? I mean, after all, Jean is clearly a saint and you are especially open. These things can't happen to others, can they?"

To repeat myself, yes, they can. When you open your heart and mind, you will discover that your loved ones are constantly trying to make contact with you. To be receptive to spirit presence, you must cultivate awareness. As you make a conscious decision to do that, you will be amazed by how quickly your senses are unlocked and set free.

A deep spirituality is the final factor that enables the communion Jean and I now share. I have realized that Jean was a mystic who was in constant energetic communication with God and the spirit realm. In retrospect, I see how often he intervened on my behalf.

For example, one day when I had a terrible headache, he prayed to Fluffy, our beloved canary who had died a couple of years before. I didn't realize at the time that he chose to pray to Fluffy because he knew that the spirit of our bird was in communion with God and the saints. Jean was speaking to God through our little feathered emissary. As soon as he prayed, my headache disappeared.

Another day, I told Jean, "I miss Fluffy." He said, "I know, Jamie." I went upstairs to the laundry room, where the window beside the dryer was open. Suddenly a bird landed on the windowsill. I leaned my cheek against the screen and the bird kissed my cheek, then my nose, just as Fluffy used to do. Jean had obviously called the spirit of my bird to reach out to me through the wild bird. I came downstairs and said to him, "You won't believe what just happened." I didn't need to tell him the story. He simply said, "I know, Jamie."

Even more directly, when I had a fever that wouldn't break for days, Jean put his hand on mine and silently prayed. I fell into a trancelike sleep, and when I awoke the fever was magically gone.

After Jean left his body, I studied his photos and noticed that he always had an otherworldly expression, as if he wasn't fully of the earth. As I mentioned, he walked with a weightless, ethereal quality, and always had a radiant glow to his skin, as though he were lit from within.

He was perpetually serene, as if he saw a world that no one else saw. It never occurred to me until after his death that he was already partially in the spirit realm, not fully in a human body even though he still lived on earth.

As for me, in hindsight I realize that the seeds of spirituality had lain dormant inside me, waiting to be cultivated by my union with Jean. Throughout our life together, Jean was a daily witness to my experiments with energetic communication. We were both aware that humans have a tremendous, often untapped power that emanates from the proper channeling of energy. Our thoughts are energy; *we* are energy.

Consider when you're stopped at a red light and look over at the driver in the car next to yours. Why does the other driver always seem to look back at you? I believe it's because the person has picked up the energetic frequency of your gaze. Similarly, I always seem to know who is calling when the phone rings. This is another example of receiving energetic signals. Some people refer to it as extrasensory perception (ESP).

The same mechanism occurs in reverse when we energetically communicate a desire or intention. This happened recently with a journalist who interviewed me five years ago for WebMD. Although I hadn't spoken to her since, I wanted to do another interview with her but couldn't find either her phone number or e-mail address. So I sent a message to her energetically, and the *very next day*, she e-mailed me. She said I popped into her mind and she thought that it would be good to interview me after so much time had passed. This was obviously no coincidence.

Communicating with Animals

Some of my most magical and divine experiences occur when I communicate energetically with any kind of animal. Jean and I conducted many observational experiments and concluded that animals understand and respond to my communications because I'm somehow attuned to their frequency and transmit brainwaves they're able to process.

One day in spring, Jean and I visited Bartholomew's Cobble, an outdoor park featuring tiny bright wildflowers cascading down from rock walls and boulders.

When we arrived, the woods were silent. I told Jean, "Today I'm going to call the birds to us, species by species."

He gave me a look of extreme skepticism.

I then proceeded to sing, "Little titmouse. Little titmouse . . ." In a few moments, a titmouse appeared on the branch above us. It tweeted hello to us in its hoarse, raspy voice.

Jean was flabbergasted.

I next called the chickadee. In seconds, a chickadee appeared above us, dancing on a branch, singing "chick-a-dee."

Then I called for a cardinal, and in no time a beautiful apricot-colored female materialized before us.

Jean, the ultraspiritualist, was astounded. We concluded that while these creatures surely don't know the English names of their respective species, they understood on an energetic level when I called out to each of them.

Similarly, during Easter week one year, I espied a cage in which there were three bunnies—a white one, a yellow one, and a black one. With no hand gestures, I said, "Yellow bunny, hop over here and kiss my cheek." The yellow one did. Next I told the black one to come and kiss me, and he complied! Then, at my summons, the white one did the same.

Jean was shocked.

Just recently, I took a walk and a rabbit stopped beside me. I said to him, "I love you."

In response, he wiggled his mouth three times, obviously repeating the three words I had just spoken.

In the summer of 2005, at the Nice airport on the French Riviera, I saw a large aquarium. Walking up to it, I designated a specific fish out of thousands and told Jean that I would ask that fish to swim over and snuggle next to my cheek. It did.

Just before leaving for our final vacation together, we visited the Silvermine Tavern, a charming old Connecticut inn perched high above a waterfall. When we arrived, I took a walk into a wooded area beyond a rushing stream and soon came upon a male and female cardinal. The two birds excitedly chirped, danced at my feet, and wiggled their beaks once or twice in response to my words *hi* and *hello*. They also audibly mimicked the sound of my voice when I said "Hi." They stayed with me for more than an hour, and even after it had grown dark, they refused to leave me.

I finally told them, "It's not safe for you to stay up any longer. I'll give you both names—Candy and Chuck. I promise to come back tomorrow. When I do, I'll call your names. Then you can fly back to me." They obeyed and flew away.

The next day, I asked Jean to walk with me back to that wooded area. We crossed a stream, and when I was where I had been the previous day, I called out, "Candy and Chuck, I'm back. Come to me."

In the distance, very far away, I heard the cardinals' flight song. It took some minutes for them to return from where they were, but come to me they did.

During one of our last vacations in France, Jean and I saw a brace of ducks. I said aloud, in English, "I've never spoken to ducks before. If you understand me, open your bills once and say 'hi' to me." Just as the cardinals in the woods had done, the ducks opened their bills once to imitate the way my mouth opened when I spoke to them. Several of them even mimicked the word *hi* with a guttural greeting.

Jean concluded that because they were French ducks that had never heard English before, they understood me only because they were picking up energetic signals from my brain.

To test this theory, I told Jean on another occasion, "I'm going to silently tell the bird sitting next to me to wiggle his beak twice, to say 'hello.'" Sure enough, I sent the thought and the bird did just what I had silently requested.

A Glimpse of Heaven

Communicating energetically with animals (or people) offers a glimpse of how spirit beings communicate telepathically. Heaven is a great melting pot where spirits from all over the world are united as one family. When these beings lived in human form, they spoke the languages of their countries of origin. But in spirit form, energetic communication is the universal language.

In fact, I now believe animals are more evolved than humans since they can send and receive energetic communications as a matter of course. Think about how a robin knows exactly where to dig in order to find an earthworm. Clearly, the worm is emitting energetic signals that the robin perceives! Birds also know to flee a region even before our detection equipment registers an earthquake is about to occur. Likewise, seagulls fly well inland long before a major storm such as a hurricane hits a coastal region.

Oddly enough, even flies seem to understand my energetic communications. Whenever I tell them to come into my hand so that I can take them outside, they fly willingly to me. Recently, a patient of mine named Candi watched as a fly allowed me to take it between my thumb and index finger and carry it outside.

On many occasions, Jean and I communicated energetically while he still lived in a body. For example, each time I thought about wanting him to take me out to dinner at a specific restaurant, he would call soon afterward and tell me that he'd just made a reservation at that very place.

Energy, Healing, and the Physical World

Jean and I also came to understand my ability to lay hands on people and heal their ailments as simply the ability to direct energy with a healing intention. Throughout my life, I've made it a practice to help anyone who crosses my path who is sick or in pain, including friends, family members, acquaintances, and even strangers. More recently, it has come to feel unethical *not* to offer healing assistance to my patients when they're sick or in pain. As a consequence, I've consciously chosen to do healings on my patients when they are in need.

As I mentioned, I've also discovered that I can transmit energy so that healings can occur without touch, at long distances. What I do in these cases is sit down, close my eyes, take a deep breath, and, as I exhale, I consciously send a burst of what I can only describe as a white light to the person in need.

For example, several years ago, Alexandre, Jean's brother-in-law living in France, was given the last rites. I sent a burst of healing energy to him all the way from America; I felt a jolt when it hit. His family called later that day and said he had miraculously recovered.

I have offered similar healings to friends and patients throughout my life, often with the same astonishing results.

Strange as it sounds, Jean also watched me turn streetlights on and off at will. He assumed that I was acting upon the particular energetic frequency that operates the lights.

On our last trip to Cape May, New Jersey, Jean and I sat in a restaurant's screened-in outdoor patio. In the distance was a row of commercial streetlights. I selected one of the lights and told him that when I turned to face it, it would turn off. It did. Then I told him that when I turned away, it would come back on. It did.

As people at surrounding tables were commenting on the strange way the light was operating, Jean and I laughed at our private joke. I did the operation about 20 times in a row. Finally, I suggested that he try. He'd never attempted this before and doubted that he would succeed. But after a minute of concentrating, he was able to do the same thing.

I firmly believe that communicating with a spirit being is no different from what I have already described. If you are with me thus far, then you're ready to move on to creating a state of receptivity and using that knowledge to connect with loved ones in the spirit world.

PART III

Learning to Connect with Spirit

CHAPTER 13

∞∿◇∿

CREATING YOUR OWN
STATE OF RECEPTIVITY

∞∿◇∿

Grieving tears open your being
Making you more open to seeing

Now that you know that love has no barriers—that it tran-
scends time, space, and alternate dimensions—you're ready to create your own state of receptivity.

In this chapter, I'll teach you the skills you need to send and
receive spirit communications. Your ability to communicate with
spirit is a two-pronged process. First you need to turn your entire
being into a receiver that is in tune with the communications that
are being sent to you. But a receiver in the full "on" position isn't
enough. All your sensory organs also need to be acutely attuned so
that you can see, hear, smell, taste, and feel these communications.

There are several ways to tune up your receiver. The first is
internal cleansing, fasting, and heating the body with saunas and
fevers. While nobody relishes being sick, it's widely known in the
alternative health community that fevers are to be welcomed and
embraced for their cleansing and healing abilities. I have even

heard of cases in which people are spontaneously cured of cancer by one incident of high fever. The point is, when we're "lucky" enough to come down with a fever, allow the body to ride it out rather than trying to suppress it using over-the-counter medicines. Of course, do seek medical attention for especially high or prolonged fevers, or as necessary to be safe, depending on the individual situation.

In addition, in this chapter I will share five more methods for increasing your receptivity: (1) cultivating the ability to be truly still and quiet; (2) surrendering to all your emotional states; (3) entering a trance by bypassing your conscious mind through meditation, progressive relaxation, self-hypnosis, prayer, yoga, Tai Chi, Chi Gong, and/or deep-breathing; (4) experiencing hypnagogic (twilight) states; and (5) using nature.

Finally, to cultivate heightened awareness, I will share various exercises for awakening your sensory and psychic abilities.

Before we proceed, a word of caution: I spoke earlier about the shameful way our Western society and medical establishment handle the grieving process. As I indicated before, if people haven't "snapped out of it" in a few months, doctors are quick to prescribe antidepressants. While grief may mimic the symptoms of depression, it is not the same thing. Beware of taking such drugs because they will blunt your capacity to be open to your feelings and senses. The numbing effect of these medications can interfere with your receptivity. Moreover, as I've observed in many patients with whom I've shared my methodology, the process of reconnecting has the power to lift sadness in ways that drugs can't begin to address. So beware of taking drugs unless absolutely necessary. (Of course, it's important to discuss discontinuing any medication with your doctor rather than stopping cold turkey, and those suffering from depression should definitely seek treatment.)

Cultivating the Ability to Be Still and Quiet

When communicating with spirit beings, your first order of business is to create what I refer to as "pockets of peace." I discovered this requirement as soon as I returned from Italy without Jean. Within the first week, I was guided to turn off my television and every other electronic device. Without consciously realizing it, I was being advised to sit in silence so that I could hear Jean.

One night Jean implanted this thought in my head: *My little darling, don't be afraid of being alone in the dark. It is in the silence that you will hear my voice. The conversation and the noise of the day drown out my voice. Any time you want to talk to me, come to the bed, be still, and you will hear me. It is in the quiet that we will always unite.*

The morning after this communication, I spoke with my friend Ann Flynn, a devout Catholic. I told her that Jean told me about seeking silence in order to hear him. She then quoted for me what the Bible says: "Be still and know that I am God."

It was thus in silence that I soon came to live in a nearly constant state of meditation. Since a primary purpose of meditation is to be one with God and spirit by turning off the conscious part of the mind, the more you're still and quiet, the more in touch you will be with spirit.

Since I tend to do everything to the extreme, I adopted the practice of being very still and quiet during every moment I wasn't working with patients. Now I'm not saying that you must convert your condo into a convent. Just cultivate your own "pockets of peace"—moments in which you tune out the world and turn down your conscious mind. When your conscious mind is quiet, your brain is able to perceive what it cannot hear during the daily humdrum of ordinary activity. In this state, you are supremely open to spirit and God. In this state, you can soar beyond your earthly body, travel to alternate dimensions, and unite with beings in the spirit realm. (You may have heard this phenomenon referred to as an out-of-body experience or OBE.) The ultimate goal of being still and quiet is to clear your mind and empty your vessel so you can receive signs, messages, and the eternal love that spirit holds for you.

I know this is easier said than done because our Western lifestyle rarely condones a state of stillness. We're all overworked, always rushing somewhere, and never still until we sleep at night— and then our rest is often fitful as a result of the day's stress. Later in this chapter, I will provide instructions and guidelines for meditation and other peaceful practices.

Surrendering to All Your Emotional States

In addition, many people try to defuse their anxieties by becoming workaholics, shopaholics, and/or alcoholics. Millions more resort to unhealthy or excessive sex, eating, drug use, gambling, and even hobbies. While these sorts of activities may permit us to temporarily escape unpleasant feelings, their long-term effects can be debilitating if not disastrous. More to the point, they block receptivity.

By contrast, for years I have tended to openly acknowledge my feelings and not back away from pain. The period after Jean left his body was no exception. Although in agony during those days, weeks, and months, I discovered that pain is a purgative that opens our vessel. It literally breaks us down emotionally and physically to lift us up spiritually. Perhaps this explains why those who chronically suffer from physical and emotional ailments are often better equipped to hear spirit. While I'm not advocating illness or pain for anyone at any point, the fact remains that life does deliver some hard blows from time to time. These troubles have side benefits we can embrace.

If you want to open your vessel (that is, your mind and body) to send and receive communications with spirit, don't run away or bury your feelings in soul-numbing or distracting behaviors. Starting today, vow to flex your emotional muscles and train yourself to tolerate all your feelings, positive and negative alike. I realize that what I'm proposing here is not a natural act for everyone. I therefore encourage you to approach it like training at the gym. When you first start a new regimen, your muscles are weak and you can't bear a lot of weight. But with time and practice, your muscles develop. You become stronger and can bear more and more weight. The psyche works in much the same way. As you ask yourself to bear more and more emotional weight, its "muscles" become stronger and more able to tolerate intense feelings. The following poem that I wrote just after Jean left his body sums up this point.

BE LIKE A WILLOW

I allow the storm of emotions to wash over me
Like a gracefully bending willow tree

I invite you to make these words your new mantra. As you surrender to your emotional storms and allow the rough waters to crest over you, this pain will create miracles in your life and in the lives of others. As you will discover, intense emotions can cleanse your soul. The gift on the other side of this journey is a vessel that's open to receive boundless love from the spirit realm. As you allow it to fill you, it will naturally overflow onto others. As you pour love upon others, you will feel utterly blessed and surrounded by the light of love.

Emotional Blocks to Spirit

While being open to your feelings heightens receptivity, it's only part of the equation. Paradoxically, intense emotions block receptivity, so you also must be careful to keep yourself in check. The engulfing grief and anger that often mark the early stages of loss can dead bolt your heart and deafen your ability to hear.

I can attest to the fact that whenever I was too consumed with grief, I couldn't hear Jean speaking to me. I felt as though I were shut down and cut off from him, and therefore was unreceptive to his words. At times like these, I learned to walk a tightrope in which I was aware of the extent of my grief but not drowning in it. When I was this upset, I gave myself what I call a "*Moonstruck* moment." Do you remember the scene in the movie *Moonstruck* when Nicolas Cage declares his love to Cher, who is engaged to marry his brother? She doesn't want to hear that he loves her, so she slaps him and says, "Snap out of it!" So whenever I found myself on the verge of emotional flooding, I said this to myself and, in so doing, I snapped myself out of self-pity and back into a state of receptivity.

The question arises, How can you be open to all emotional experiences while at the same time avoiding what I describe as "emotional flooding"? First, you need to cultivate the ability to consciously observe yourself. To do this, you must fortify a part of the psyche that's called the observing ego. One way to strengthen the observing ego's power to step back and watch the self with a degree of detachment is to imagine yourself split in two. One part of you is sitting in the corner, at the edge of the ceiling, and looking down upon the other part. Another way to awaken your observing ego is to imagine yourself like an eagle, watching yourself from above. As you observe yourself, you must learn to recognize the signs that you're on the verge of emotionally flooding. These signs include a feeling of being washed overboard, out of control, or hysterical. You might find yourself crying uncontrollably, unable to catch your breath. Or you might be yelling or screaming. When you're flooding, you aren't watching your feelings; you are drowning in them.

As your observing ego grows stronger, you can learn to regulate your own emotional states. Consider a radio volume dial. You can turn the knob up or down. Likewise, with the help of your observing ego, you will learn to recognize when you're starting to flood and cultivate the ability to be emotionally aware without becoming overwhelmed.

In addition, I've discovered that common attitudes and beliefs that we have in response to our suffering can actually block receptivity to spirit. It is important for us to understand the role that suffering plays in our lives and how it's linked to our spiritual development. Having the right perspective can help us to not fall prey to the feelings of bitterness, sadness, and hopelessness that bog down most grieving people. These feelings dead bolt our hearts and prevent us from receiving spirit.

In the next section, I'm going to offer you a brief overview of the messages that Jean shared with me regarding suffering. It is my hope that this newfound understanding will help you open your heart to spirit.

Spirit Can't Prevent Our Struggles

While Jean has shown me that he's holding me in my pain, he has also taught me that he can't bundle me in bubble wrap or stop me from experiencing the struggles that are an integral part of my journey. Hard as it is to accept, our personal growth and spiritual development often require us to experience custom-tailored trials that are designed to teach us specific spiritual lessons. When you can't pray your way out of these tight spots (and when loved ones in spirit can't remove the challenge), it is likely because life is happening to you just the way it is meant to.

So when desperate measures to wiggle out of a tight spot fail, instead of falling into a state of bitterness or despair, consider that you may be encountering a spiritual lesson in disguise. In my case, my uncontrollable weight taught me that I must surrender the illusion of control and accept that I don't have power over many things. For a vain and driven person like me, surrendering has been, by far, the hardest reality to accept.

The Soil of Spiritual Growth

Why is surrendering the illusion of control so important to our spiritual development?

As I discovered the hard way, when we're smacked by the tsunamis of life, we're being asked to bow to forces greater than ourselves. Physical and emotional suffering, including grief, serve to break down our defenses. Our souls must be open in order to hear God and spirit. When sorrowful things happen, we can either become bitter and petulant or view these trials as the gift that brings us closer to God and the spirit realm. It is said that the heart must be broken again and again in order to finally be opened. Only when our heart is open can we hear God and spirit calling us to perfect our ability to love others better.

Learning Gratitude

As I reflected further on the suffering that life brings, I realized that we cannot appreciate the light if we never see the darkness. Similarly, how can we know joy except by contrast? When we suffer, we're being taught to appreciate the simple gratitude that comes when the pain stops. Remember, we can't appreciate light without living in the dark.

Empathy for Others

My housekeeper and friend, Donna, continually tells me that I've become much kinder since Jean left his body. Great pain enables us to empathize with others who suffer. Undergoing our own trials trains us to be more Godlike and loving, and to understand, empathize, and connect to others in their pain.

God's Chosen

It's been revealed to me that those who grieve, as well as the sick, the dying, the disabled, and those who emotionally suffer, are God's chosen ones. They are sacrificial lambs, sent by God to instill a sense of gratitude in other people. Those who suffer are chosen to spark others to fulfill their universal mission on earth, which is to be more Godlike, kinder, more loving, more empathic, and more giving—in other words, to grow as spiritual beings. Of course, when a sufferer receives your kindness, he or she is also receiving God's blessing. In this way both the giver and the receiver are blessed.

Those who suffer the most are God's agents in yet another way. Consider the simple fact that a certain percentage of unemployment is built in to a capitalist economy. People who don't work are serving society by keeping things churning along. This is because, according to economists, the capitalist economy cannot function with a 100 percent employment rate. Human suffering works in a similar fashion. When we suffer, we are being chosen to serve humanity! I know this is an unusual perspective, but stay with me. When we see someone in pain, we're being invited to stop feeling sorry for ourselves and give thanks for the problems we have that pale in comparison. Another person's difficulty reminds us that we could have it much worse.

A spiritual friend of mine once said that he doesn't like the idea of taking solace in another person's suffering. I am not advocating a smug or superior reaction in which we sit back and rest on our emotional laurels. On the contrary! Another person's distress is an invitation to get out of ourselves and focus on others, to stop dwelling on our own worries and instead do whatever we can to make life better for someone who is worse off than we are. Remember: When we throw ourselves a pity party, there is always someone out there who has it far worse and who desperately needs our prayers and assistance.

Becoming Close to God

When we're in the darkest moments of our lives, in terrible pain, frightened, and feeling completely forsaken by spirit, it's easy to fall into a pit of despair. In reality, difficult as it is to believe, it's at these times that we're actually closest to God!

Why? Just as when a parent teaches a child a hard lesson, it is spirit that stands beside you and supports you even as it puts the tough lesson before you. In reality, suffering is a sign of God's presence, not absence! When you look at your suffering in this way, you can actually feel grateful for the time God devotes to helping you grow spiritually.

Remember that each trial you face is a spiritual lesson in disguise. You can feel like a victim and become depressed and turn your back on spirit, or you can remind yourself that everything happens for a reason. When you approach challenges with this attitude, you will then naturally ask yourself what your current difficulty is teaching you, and how you can share this lesson with others to make the world a better place.

Receiving What We Need at Each Moment

I'm sure you've heard it said, "God never gives you more than you can handle." This statement is designed to help people weather the tough times, but I think it needs to be revised. We aren't supposed to white-knuckle our way through life. When we have a hard time, we're supposed to open our hearts, eyes, and ears and decipher what this hard time is teaching us. We are given exactly what we need in order to complete our spiritual development. When life is painful, think of it as spiritual growing pains, or that hair is being put on your spiritual chest!

Testing Our Faith

It's easy to have faith during the good times. But can you keep the faith and not give up hope even when you're lost in the desert? Can you keep believing that your loved ones and God are with you even when you feel utterly alone and forsaken?

After Jean's death, I was given great gifts, including health improvements and miraculous weight loss—gifts that instantly created faith in me that the afterlife and God do, indeed, exist. By granting me the gift of being thin, Jean instantly infused me with a deep faith. No other earthly intervention had ever worked to help me lose weight. Faith came easily in the face of such a miracle.

Then, as I described earlier in the book, I was forced to face a series of new trials. At one point or another each miracle was temporarily taken. Each time I experienced a setback, I felt depressed and terrified that both Jean and God had left me. I was being tested big time!

For me, the greatest trial of all was regaining all the water weight. My worst nightmare was upon me. Among other things, my faith was being pushed to its limits! I was being tested to see if I could keep my belief when the gifts were removed. Did I have sufficient trust in my heart that Jean and God were still present in my life, despite the apparent evidence to the contrary? It was there, in the heart of darkness, that I finally understood what Jean meant when he told me soon after his death, *Have faith in faith and trust in trust. Open your heart and believe.*

Naturally, when my body began holding water weight again, I felt forsaken—a common reaction when life deals us a bad hand. I'm sure you've heard people say, or you've said yourself, "How could God have done this to me?" or "How could God have allowed this to happen?" Of course, we say these things because we've forgotten that our trials are spiritual lessons in disguise. In our hurt and anger, we turn away from God and our loved ones in spirit.

Realizing this, I took a leap of faith and trusted that Jean was and is with me even in the darkest hours. As soon as I made this shift in perspective, the fire of his love once again entered me fully (and became my own self-love, too). At that moment, I began losing weight again!

This experience has led me to conclude that our physical imbalances and diseases can often be a sign of spiritual "dis-ease." When a physical symptom doesn't resolve (despite affirmations, visualizations, and prayers), that may mean that we haven't yet mastered the spiritual lesson. When the lesson is conquered, the symptom is often resolved.

But in some cases, the symptom may not resolve during our earthly ride. This isn't because we're being punished or because we aren't visualizing or doing our affirmations properly. Rather, there are cases in which our physical and emotional symptoms aren't meant to be resolved because they may be required to help us fulfill our spiritual development. In the case of Padre Pio, for example, in 1918 he experienced his first occurrence of the stigmata, in which his body exhibited marks, pain, and bleeding at the location of Christ's crucifixion wounds. It is reported that he was embarrassed by these wounds and prayed to God to remove them. But the affliction continued for 50 years, until his death. Magically, the wounds closed within hours of his death, and his body was empty of blood.

The point is that there are so many mysteries. And because mysteries are of the Divine, they can't be fully fathomed by the human mind. In my case, Jean has told me that I'm living in a human body that is particularly sensitive to stress. That means that I am always prone to gaining weight when life is tough.

Perhaps my spiritual lesson is to let go and accept that which I don't want to accept. At the same time, because my body is my barometer, my water weight can be a sign of my lost connection with the boundless love of spirit. Whenever I see myself starting to hold water, I know that I'm disconnected. When I reconnect to spirit and Jean's love for me, which is my love of myself, my body melts again.

Ultimately, the fire of love is the cure for what ails us. Having a greater awareness of our emotions and how we respond to suffering allows us to better access spirit, and the love waiting there for us.

Using a Trance to Bypass Your Conscious Mind

There are various activities and practices such as prayer, meditation, yoga, Tai Chi, Chi Gong, self-hypnosis, visualization, progressive relaxation, and deep breathing that enable you to calm your body and mind and create the calm and mental clarity that permits you to enter a trance state.

When you're in a trance, your mind is more finely attuned and your psychic abilities are humming at a higher level. In fact, when your conscious mind is turned off, you have access to a part of the brain called the superconscious mind. This is the source of all power, knowledge, love, and peace. The superconscious mind is also free from the constraints of time and space—in other words, it has no limitations. When you enter this place, you can more easily connect with loved ones in spirit.

Recognizing When You're in a Trance

Now, I don't want you to think of a trance as some exotic state of mind that only mystics sitting on mountaintops can achieve. In reality, we humans enter trances at various points throughout the day. For example, when was the last time you became distracted while you were driving, and the next thing you knew, you were miles beyond your exit? Or maybe you've found yourself so engrossed in a book, movie, or conversation that the passage of hours felt like mere minutes. At such times, whether you realized it or not, you were in a trance.

The sensations associated with a trance state differ from person to person. In general, you'll know that you're there when you feel deeply relaxed and peaceful. Your respiration and heart rate will slow down. You may feel like you're groggy or drowsy, but you won't be asleep. You'll find that your "monkey mind" will become still to the point that you stop flitting mentally from branch to branch. Everyday thoughts and concerns will give way to a heightened state of awareness.

Exercises for Entering a Trance

In this next section, I share some exercises I have developed to help you enter a trance. For some people, meditation is the portal to paradise. For others, physical postures (such as those associated with yoga or Tai Chi), deep breathing, or visualizations are most effective in initiating a trance. I advise you to experiment with each of these possibilities until you determine which one works best for you.

Meditation Made Simple

One night soon after Jean passed, he told me, *Whenever you want to connect with me, use your breath to draw me inside your body.* I inhaled deeply, and he was there! I can't really explain how I knew. It was one of the many pieces of channeled wisdom that entered me, and I just knew. The experience goes entirely outside of textbook learning. And it was then that I understood that spirit is borne on the breath. This surely explains why all meditation practices revolve around breathing.

To begin your meditation, choose a private place where you won't be disturbed for at least an hour, although you may find

121

that you want to extend your practice to several hours at a time. As you become more proficient at meditating, you'll ease into a trance in less and less time. Eventually you may require only 15 or 20 minutes to enter into a deep trance.

Choose a position in which you feel comfortable, but don't lie down. You don't want to fall asleep! Sitting on a comfortable cushion with your legs loosely crossed or sitting in a chair are the most common positions. The important thing is to choose a posture that feels right for you.

You can opt to play relaxing music if it helps you focus your mind. Some prefer silence. In either case, you want to sit without attempting to *do* anything; just feel your body relaxing. If you're a go-getter, you will probably find this exercise excruciatingly difficult to do, akin to watching grass grow.

Close your eyes. Be prepared for your mind to wander. Each time it does, say silently, *Thought.* Don't attach any significance to the thought; just watch it float across your mental landscape, like a balloon passing by. In fact, there's a type of meditation called "thought watching" in which you do just that for the entire session.

After 10 or 15 minutes (after your mind has quieted), begin to observe your breath.

Don't try to control your breathing. Just be aware of the air going in through your nostrils and mouth and then passing out again. As you breathe, observe the sensations taking place throughout your body. Don't judge or try to change anything; just notice how the sensations are fluctuating as time passes.

Sense your breath and your body for at least an hour. You may not achieve anything like a trance the first time you do this. Just continue to follow this practice every day and watch for the previously mentioned signs that you've entered a trance.

This is certainly not meant to be a stress-inducing activity— just the opposite! So don't worry about achieving anything right away. Just be. In time, you will fall into a trance without effort. When you finally are able to enter this state, allow yourself to do nothing but float freely and happily in it. In the next chapter, I will show you how to use this state to enable you to reconnect with loved ones in spirit.

Breath-Counting Meditation

If you find yourself being bombarded with thoughts that prevent you from quieting your mind and entering a trance, you may find this meditation helpful. Instead of just releasing thoughts, your goal is to focus the mind on counting inhalations and exhalations. As you inhale, say silently to yourself, *Inhale one*. As you exhale, say silently, *Exhale one*. The ideal is to reach the number five without a thought intruding. Don't be surprised if you don't make it that far. Some well-known mystics have taken a long time to achieve this ability. Even if you don't get to five, the advantage of this exercise is that it distracts your mind from conjuring up obsessive thoughts. In the process, you can actually trick your mind into entering a trance.

If you're the kind of person who gets antsy when you sit still and always needs to be busy, you can add one simple physical act to this meditation. While you're saying to yourself, *Inhale one*, position your tongue at the gum line just behind your two top front teeth. As you exhale and say silently, *Exhale one*, move your tongue to the gum line just behind your two bottom front teeth. Continue this alternating movement as you count to five. This added activity might be just what you need to calm your mind and settle into a trance.

Visualization to Enter a Trance

You can also use the power of your mind to visualize your way into a trance. To do this, bring into your mind an imaginary or real safe place. Such places might include a location where you felt safe as a child, like at Grandma's house baking cookies. Adult safe places might include a quiet beach cove or wherever you enjoyed the loving embrace of a best friend.

Start by lying down or sitting. Close your eyes and take three deep breaths. As you breathe, imagine a golden light entering your body through your crown chakra, the energy center located at the top of your head. With each exhalation, feel this warm golden

light wash over your body. Imagine it having the power to penetrate your blood, organs, and cells. As you exhale, feel the tension
leaving your body through your fingertips and toes. As the tension eases, feel yourself sinking deeper and deeper into the chair,
couch, or bed.

Now imagine this light pouring over you like warm lava and
melting into you. Your muscles are turning to taffy, melting under
a summer sun. See this light as it flows downward, starting from
your head, and then moving down your face, neck, shoulders,
arms, hands, fingers, chest, upper back, stomach, midback, groin,
lower back, thighs, knees, shins, calves, ankles, feet, and toes. If
you sense any areas of your body resisting the flow, visualize your
inhaling breath entering those areas of constriction and then
imagine your exhaling breath flushing out the tension.

As you continue breathing, feel yourself sinking deeper into
a state of relaxation, as if you're in a bucket being lowered into a
well or in an elevator dropping lower and lower until you reach
the state in which you're free of tension and worry.

Hypnagogic or Twilight States

In addition to meditating and visualizing, there is yet another
way to open yourself to the superconscious part of your mind. You
can take advantage of the hypnagogic state, which is the drowsy
but often highly creative period between wakefulness and sleep.
There are many other names for this, but whatever you call it, it's
the same state of mind that is activated during meditation.

While normally the transition between full wakefulness and
sleep is a brief one, it's important to realize that with practice, you
can choose to linger in this state for as long as you wish. Doing so
will open yet another doorway to spirit. You can choose to do this
in the morning or evening or even before or after napping. The
danger of doing this exercise in the evening is that you may be so
tired that you fall asleep. Not being a napper myself, I find that
early morning is ideal. Early morning is also a time of heightened
creativity for many people.

Now that you're on the path to greater receptivity, let's turn to deepening your awareness so that you can fully acknowledge all the signs that are being sent to you on a daily basis.

Testing Your Awareness

To start, let's do a little exercise for testing your awareness. You'll need a paper and pen. The next time you're in a room that you've never visited before, visually scan the space for one minute and notice everything you can. Obviously, you can't do this in your own house, since you know the environment too well. But you can try it at a friend's house or in any public location.

Leave the room after one minute and write down what you saw. If you're at a friend's house, you can explain why you're doing this exercise. This way, when you leave abruptly, your friend won't think it's something he or she said! If you're doing this exercise in a public place with strangers, your leaving will go unnoticed.

After you're finished, go back into the room and take note of what you missed. Don't despair if you overlooked a great deal. That is to be expected at first. Keep practicing and you'll be amazed by how much your awareness improves. The more aware you are, the more open your mind becomes, and thus the more skilled you will become at recognizing the energetic messages that your loved ones are sending you.

Being in the Perfect Present

I'm sure you have read or heard that mindfulness and living in the present (the "now") is the key to the end of human suffering, and of course I've already discussed it quite a bit! It's extremely important. I can't tell you how often I've seen patients who can't seem to escape the trap of bemoaning their miserable lives. They hyperfocus on terrible events in the past or obsess about what dreadful disasters await them down the road.

When I can succeed in getting them to lift the needle off the record and just be with me in the now, the most miraculous thing happens. As we abide together in a blessed state of intimate connectedness, time seems to take on a different dimension. Past and future concerns fade away. This is because when we stop worrying about the past or future, we're free to simply *be* in the present. When we settle down and focus on the current moment, we discover that this very instant is usually perfect. When one is intensely present in the perfect present, a heightened sense of awareness is achieved.

One way to cultivate being in the now is to be fully present with yourself. An easy way to do this is to focus on your breath. Feel the air entering and exiting your nostrils. Or even try imagining your breath having eyes that search out areas of physical tension. As you exhale, focus on releasing all stress.

The most important byproduct of living fully in the now is its ability to heighten your powers of awareness and silence the internal chatter that blocks receptivity. In other words, living in the now is the ultimate ongoing trance.

Nature

One of the best ways to enter the present is to commune with nature. Nature has a unique way of nudging you toward the beauty and meaning of the moment. As you gaze upon the sunset's pastel hues melting beneath the horizon or as you relish a silky breeze caressing your skin, the scent of honeysuckle wafting through the air, the nectar of a succulent peach bursting on your tongue, or the symphony of a songbird, you are fully alive—you are fully aware—in and of the moment. It is thus easy to see why nature readily induces a trance.

I recommend that you visit your favorite places in nature. Take regular walks, stroll in a nearby park, or sit on the beach. Even spending time in your backyard is a good way to allow the embrace of nature to bring you back to the now.

Heightening Your Five Senses

To receive the communications that are being sent to you from loved ones in spirit, you must finely tune your senses. A good way to stimulate your five senses is to sit in Mother Nature's lap. Let's imagine we're conducting the following exercises in a forest. Focus on attuning yourself one sense at a time. Let's start with your vision.

— **To heighten your sense of sight:** Set a timer for three minutes, close your eyes, and take three deep breaths. When you open your eyes, imagine that you're seeing the world through the eyes of a young child who's viewing the forest for the first time. Notice the silhouettes and shadows of overlapping leaves. Notice the light that peeks through the tiny pinpricks that insects have gnawed in these leaves. Notice the tiny feet of the caterpillar wriggling along the forest floor.

For the following four exercises, I encourage you to blindfold yourself. Just as a blind person develops the other senses to compensate for lack of sight, you can deprive yourself of your vision to heighten all your nonvisual senses.

— **To heighten your sense of smell:** Next, set the timer for another three minutes, close your eyes, and keep them closed (if you aren't using a blindfold). This time, focus on your sense of smell. Breathe in the crisp fragrance of pine and the cider-sweet scent of rotting leaves and ferns.

— **To heighten your sense of hearing:** Again set the timer for three minutes, close your eyes or use a blindfold, and listen to the sounds of nature. They are all around you. Hear the wind whispering through the trees and the rustling of a chipmunk scurrying through a maze of fallen leaves or the buzzing of an insect.

— **To heighten your sense of touch:** Then set the timer for another three minutes. Feel the silky, spongy moss that clings to the cold rocks. Dip your fingers into a rushing stream and feel the tingle of the icy water on your flesh.

Blindfold yourself a final time, and once again set your timer for three minutes. This time have your friend touch you with various objects of different textures. See if you can discern what types of objects are touching your skin. Can you distinguish a rock from a piece of glass or a chalkboard, a rubber eraser from a stick of gum?

— **To heighten your sense of taste:** I don't recommend you taste the forest. If you sample poison mushrooms and berries, you may find yourself in spirit form sooner than you'd like! The exercises for this sense will be easier to perform if you enlist someone to assist you.

Have a friend choose a variety of items with various scents—sweet, sour, stinky. Set a timer for ten minutes, and see how well you do at identifying each scent, since smell is so closely linked to taste.

The human palate is able to perceive five types of tastes: sweet, sour, salty, bitter, and umami, which is a pleasant savory flavor occurring naturally in many foods, as well as in monosodium glutamate. For this exercise, blindfold yourself again, set the timer for ten minutes, and have your friend offer you a smorgasbord of tastes by placing in your mouth various foods with a variety of flavors. Again, see how well you do.

To further heighten your sense of taste, from now on when you dine out, make it a point to discern every ingredient that's contained in each of the dishes placed before you.

Practice all these exercises with the enthusiasm and playful spirit of a child, and you will soon discover that all your senses are fully open to the wonder of the universe around you. As you expand your senses, you will also expand your ability to see, hear, smell, taste, and touch spirit.

Exercise for Heightening Your Psychic Abilities

In addition to heightening your sensory abilities, training your mind to expand your innate psychic abilities will further assist you in sending and receiving spirit communications.

For this next exercise, once again enlist the assistance of a friend. You will need a piece of paper and a pencil.

Choose who will be first to transmit information. That person should then write a word on a piece of paper. Choose a word that is visual, such as *sun,* as opposed to a more abstract word such as *cynical,* for which it is harder to create a mental image.

Next, the sender should concentrate on creating a mental image of the word that he or she is sending you. Set a timer for three minutes, and have the sender hold up the paper on which the word is written. Obviously, the word will be facing the sender and not the receiver. The sender should concentrate on transmitting the image via mental telepathy.

The receiver should say aloud whatever images or thoughts come to mind.

Then switch roles, with the sender becoming the receiver, and vice versa.

Keep practicing this exercise, and your psychic muscles will be in tip-top shape to send and receive spirit communications.

Meditation for Making Contact

Before I close this chapter, I want to share with you a meditation that I created to further assist you in making spirit contact. While lying in bed during a hypnagogic state (just before sleep or just upon awakening), close your eyes and breathe deeply and consciously. Fill your lungs with air. Remember, spirit is borne on the breath.

As you exhale, imagine your breath having eyes. Let the breath roam your body in search of stress or tension. Then let the breath transport the tension out of your body through your feet. Keep breathing and you will sink deeper and deeper into a meditative state. As you breathe, your body feels weighted and heavy. Imagine the sun pouring down on you, filling you with warmth and softening your muscles. Keep breathing and sinking deeper.

Now imagine your soul exiting your body, and visualize yourself floating effortlessly to where your loved one resides. Visualize the realm in any way that feels right to you. Perhaps you will see flowers, waterfalls, or ocean waves. Choose whatever image appeals to you.

In this state, you may see visions or images passing before your eyes. You may hear words or phrases. Just be open and allow the experience to penetrate you.

You may stay in this realm as long as you like. When you are ready, return to your earthly body. Open your eyes and wiggle your fingers and toes.

The more you practice this meditation, the more open you will become to visiting with loved ones in spirit.

You can also engage in this exercise while sitting in nature. It doesn't matter where you are. The key is to learn to allow yourself to enter this altered state of consciousness, to switch channels on your receiver, if you will. The more you train your brain to go to this altered state of consciousness, the easier it will be for you to return here whenever you like.

Now that your receiver is turned on and your senses are more awake, you are ready to recognize the signs of spirit presence in your life.

CHAPTER 14

RECOGNIZING THE SIGNS OF SPIRIT PRESENCE

You will find me in sleep's gentle embrace
And in the breeze that tenderly caresses your face
So when you lose your grip, reach for my hand
For I am in everyone and everywhere
Because, my love, that's how much I care

Now that your senses are heightened and your receiver is warmed up, you're primed to perceive the signs of spirit presence in your life. As I stated previously, simply becoming aware of the signs is sufficient to initiate reconnection for most people.

Bear in mind that because the signals of spirit presence are often subtle—spirit often has a way of remaining anonymous—it is easy to overlook them. So don't expect to be bowled over. On the other hand, don't be shocked or frightened if you experience astonishing displays from another realm. I certainly have.

The purpose of this chapter is to share examples of my own experiences with Jean to familiarize you with the myriad signs that spirit beings offer of their presence.

A word of warning: I don't want you to feel like an emotional orphan if your own examples don't seem as exotic or outlandish as my own. Remember, when Jean revealed my new ministry to me early on, he made it clear that he wanted me to tell our story. That is why Jean has pulled out all the stops, offering unequivocal signs to prove to the world that the spirit lives on and that love never dies. Jean is therefore not only sending signs to me. He is sending them to you as well.

So even if your signs seem subdued compared to the ones I've experienced, don't despair. You will discover that your loved ones have, nevertheless, been working up quite a sweat (imagine spirits sweating!) to signal their presence to you all along. You're also going to see that your loved ones are continually sprinkling a trail of spiritual bread crumbs to let you know that they're not only watching over you, but also yearning to continue a relationship with you. They offer these signs to remind you that they stand ready to do whatever they can to support you as you travel down life's bumpy roads. They're here to assist you in completing your spiritual growth so that you may fulfill your divine purpose on earth in preparation for your next life in spirit.

Amazingly, as I was writing this chapter on signs, a friend of mine told me that she had just heard a radio show in which a Harvard psychiatrist was discussing the grieving process. In his discussion, he referred to patients who reported receiving signs from a deceased loved one. He said that signs are nothing more than a diagnostic indicator that tells the clinician that the grieving process has not been completed. And when the grief is resolved, the signs will cease to manifest themselves. What folly! What ignorance! As you will soon discover, witnesses were often present to observe Jean's signs. These witnesses didn't know Jean and therefore were not mourning his loss. Obviously they were not in a grieving process at all!

One more point: There's an emerging field of study in which scientists are examining the question of soul survival. Some researchers are now beginning to postulate that the soul is an entity that cannot be destroyed, and that at the moment of bodily death, the soul returns to the universe at large. While this emerging science is progress, if I grasp this paradigm, it seems that scientists believe that the energy that constitutes a soul just hangs around like ethereal soap scum. As you will see from my examples, beings in spirit form are more than a residue. They are sentient beings who are completely aware and conscious of what's happening in your world, as their signs indicate!

On a general note, I want to remind you that when a loved one is no longer confined to the limitations of the body, the soul is released and free to soar. Being pure energy, spirits can influence the material world in astonishing ways that defy time, space, gravity, and the laws of science. The ways spirit can influence the material world are infinite, and the following examples demonstrate many of the most common phenomena.

Symbolic After-Death Communications (ADCs)

Spirit beings often use a symbol that either represents them or was meaningful to you both during their physical life with you. Jean chooses to talk to me through chipmunks, birds, and rabbits. The father of one of my patients uses the Cooper's hawk, which is a bird that signifies his strong essence.

Butterflies and feathers are also a common form of symbolic communication. For example, a year or so after Jean's bodily departure, I was driving one day and missing him terribly. When I pulled over, a butterfly landed on my windshield—and it stayed with me as I drove off again!

Soon around this time, I gave my first public talk about our story. As I was leaving the building after my speech in the company of the pastor who had arranged the event, we got lost and ended up in a dead-end corridor. At the end of that corridor, I noticed a poster for an old art exhibit at Vassar, featuring an etching called *The Three Trees*. I was dumbfounded. Jean's family coat of arms was called *Les Trois Arbres,* French for "the three trees"! As I walked to my car, a butterfly fluttered beside me.

Waves of Love

Because beings in spirit are one with God and because God is love, you will often experience an overpowering wave of love when a spirit comes to you. You've already read quite a few of my own examples of this earlier in the book. Here's yet another: I was driving home one day, when I suddenly felt a tidal wave of love. I then heard Jean say, *Don't worry. It will be fine.* I had no idea what he meant. One second later, I was pulling into my driveway. As I put the key in the front door, I was shocked to see that the key wouldn't turn. Once again, Jean showed me that he knew what would soon be happening to me with the lock (meaning he was seeing into the future that had already happened?). At that moment, my landscaper happened to be driving by. I flagged him down and he helped me get into the house!

Odd Physical Sensations

When a spirit is present, you may feel odd physical sensations or not feel quite like yourself. You may feel a sense of pressure or weight upon you, a sense of heat or fire, a warm glow, or a surge of energy, especially in a part of your body that needs healing. You may also experience a golden light pouring over you, a flash of deep love or ecstasy, chills up your spine, drafts or a temperature change in the room, a gust of wind rushing through you, and even goose bumps on your skin. You may also have the sensation that a spirit is touching you, as I have had on numerous occasions.

Each time Jean or another spirit presence enters me, I instantly sprout goose bumps and feel a chill running up my spine.

Physical Miracles

Spirit can act upon the world around you in miraculous ways. For weeks I had been annoyed by the dripping of the laundry-room sink. I sensed that Jean knew that it was bugging me. When I entered the laundry room one morning, the dripping was magically gone.

Another day, I was frustrated over the cord of my vacuum cleaner, which wouldn't retract back into the machine. It was like a long gray strand of spaghetti that kept tripping me. I took the machine in for service and was told that the clip inside the machine was broken and there was no way to fix the problem. The next day when I used the vacuum, I sensed that Jean had created yet another miracle. Sure enough, I pulled the spring-held mechanism, and the cord retracted like a charm.

Electronic Love Notes

Spirit beings will use whatever means are available to let you know they're present; to reassure you that they're aware of your thoughts, feelings, needs, and wishes; and to convey messages to you. Because spirits are pure energy, they easily affect electronic devices. When this happens, electronic items and lights may turn on or off. For example, I recently had a flood in the addition to my house. At the end of the day, I turned off every light and left it in the care of a team of contractors. That night, when I returned home, the chandelier in the addition was ablaze. Since Jean often uses lights to signal his presence, it made sense to me that he illuminated the chandelier in this room, because it was the one that had been destroyed by the flood. This was Jean's way of telling me that he was supporting me in the flood repair, as in all aspects of my life. And when I checked with the contractors, they confirmed that the chandelier was off when they left the house.

A Radio Wave Hello

I've heard stories of loved ones in spirit broadcasting their presence by playing a particular song at a significant moment or by making the radio volume go up or down on its own. Jean has often given me similar signs using CD players. Even though spirit beings are one with God and the saints, they still retain their unique essence. Jean was always impish, and he continues to be impish in spirit form. To this day, whenever I visit my New Jersey massage therapist, I hear Jean telling me that he's going to turn the music on and off on her CD player or raise and lower the volume. He does this until the massage therapist and I are both laughing.

Pennies from Heaven

Jean has often shown me that spirit beings can materialize objects out of thin air to signal their presence. On the six-year anniversary of Jean's passing, I was speaking with a patient named Kyla. I told her that Jean continues to send me coins that were minted in the year we were married.

As soon as I said this, she blinked and said, "I almost forgot. The other day, I was standing in the middle of the room when a coin appeared out of thin air and landed in my boot. Something told me that it was meant for you, so I kept it there."

She stood and tipped over her boot to release the coin. As she did, I heard Jean say that this coin was minted in 2006, the year that he passed. She handed me the coin. I grabbed my glasses, and sure enough, it had been minted in 2006! Pay attention to the date on any coin you find, and to any object in your path that seems out of place.

Birds of a Feather

One day, I was on the phone with my Connecticut-based former massage therapist Maureen, who knew Jean and me from the days when she used to give me massages in my house. She called me to say that she had felt Jean's presence while she was at Petco. She'd felt Jean leading her to the bird atrium, where she saw a bird that looked like Fluffy, our beloved pet canary that we had to put down a few years earlier. She walked up to the bird and said, "I have a friend named Jamie who had a canary named Fluffy. One day, Jamie asked him to sing a little song. Being playful, Fluffy uttered a short peep. Then Jamie said to him, 'You are being silly. Sing a real song!' Then he sang his heart out." Maureen told me that she then asked the little bird to sing her a little song, and he peeped once, the same way Fluffy had done when he played that game. Then she asked him to sing a real song, and he belted out a tune just like Fluffy used to do. She called me to tell me the story and to let me know how strongly she was feeling Jean's presence.

As soon as I hung up the phone, I took a walk. As I walked, I felt my gaze being pulled to the ground. What did I see? A Petco Pals key tag right in front of my foot!

License Plates

My friend Don and his partner William recounted an astonishing story to me. One night, William had a dream in which he saw Jean sitting on a tall bar stool in a bar. When William asked him what he was doing, he said, "I'm saving a place for Jamie." When William first told this story to Don, they were leaving a restaurant. As they stepped into the parking lot, a car with a license plate that read "Jamie" passed before them.

Visions

Very often Jean and other spirit presences will reveal themselves to me in the form of visions. And since Jean has left his body, I've begun receiving frequent psychic messages during sessions. He opened the door to the spirit realm, and since then I've received a constant parade of spirit visitors, all banging down my door, as it were, in search of my assistance in helping them to bring peace to my patients. Here is just one example.

One day, a young patient named Dara came into my office feeling very sad. She told me that her dog had just died. I instantly had a vision of a yellow dog and asked her if her dog was yellow. When she said no, I thought, *I'm slipping.* But the next thing I saw was another dog showing me his two enormous front paws. When I asked Dara why this dog was showing me his two front paws, she instantly burst into tears. She said that her dog that had just died was missing his two front paws. I felt a well of tears, too.

This sign reaffirms that we are restored to perfect health in our spirit bodies! Oh, and she added that she did have a yellow dog who died years earlier. So the yellow dog that I had seen first was acting as an ambassador for the one that had just died.

Houdini

On many occasions since Jean left his body, I have seen objects move, appear, and disappear. One day I looked in dismay at the decorative wooden swing (which I'd stopped using because I wanted to avoid the ticks living in the grass) that was suspended from the limb of an ancient tree that extended over my pond. The gardener had wrapped it around the tree limb, to get it out of his way when he mowed the grass. I certainly didn't want to walk out and risk picking up a tick. At that moment, right before my eyes, I watched as the swing unwrapped itself and fell free. This sign demonstrated that Jean in spirit form is aware of my feelings and wishes, and answered them without my having to ask him.

Thought Induction

Spirits often signal their presence by entering your thoughts. When this happens, a thought that you know isn't your own will suddenly pop into your head. For example, on my first airplane trip to Florida a few months following Jean's bodily departure,

I was utterly bereft to be traveling without him. Suddenly, the thought popped into my mind that the seat next to me would remain unoccupied for the flight because he was sitting in it. A few moments later, the flight attendant announced over the public address system that since the flight was overbooked, passengers should make sure to remove all personal belongings from all seats. To my astonishment, despite the overbooking, the seat beside me was never taken! I knew that this was a sign from Jean that he was flying beside me.

As I spoke with the woman in the remaining spot in our three-seat row configuration, she told the story of her life. Among other things, she said that after losing her husband, she found another great love even though she was older (was Jean reassuring me of what was coming down the pike?). And, to further put his stamp on the sign, the woman's surname was French, and the same as many of Jean's relatives.

Using Nature's Open Vessels

When you're outdoors, spirits will often give signs of their presence through animals because they are readily available tools and because they're Open Vessels.

For example, on my return from that first trip to Florida, I was feeling despondent about returning home without Jean. Just before my departure, while the plane was still stationary, I saw a bug fly past my window. I sensed that the bug was meant for me. Suddenly, it doubled back and landed on my window. I looked closely and saw that it was not one bug, but two bugs, and they were mating! Jean was telling me that we're mated for eternity. He reached me in this simple and exquisite way using the only vehicle that he could find at that moment.

When an animal is being used to signal a spirit's presence, you'll notice that the creature behaves out of character. If it's a bird, it may remain very still, sitting on a branch and not flying for a long time. Its eyes may close, and it may appear as if it's in a trance. It may sit beside you or follow you.

Spirits will often use birds and insects that fly to indicate their presence. Because they are by their nature mobile, these creatures are naturally adapted to being where spirit wants them to be at a given moment. Just as I was writing this passage, in front of the open kitchen-door window, two robins landed before me. They sat side by side on the rose arbor, looking like a couple seated shoulder to shoulder. They sat motionless in this position until I registered the message that Jean sits by my shoulder morning, noon, and night.

Using Human Open Vessels

Spirits will often offer signs of their presence using human Open Vessels. Children are naturally open. In addition, people who are disabled and even the homeless can be more open if their struggles have torn down their walls. The terminally ill and the elderly are often more open because they're closer to death and the spirit realm.

Spirit beings will use these messengers (even strangers) to comfort you. For example, in the fall of 2013, my septic system had suddenly failed and I was distressed by the prospect of a considerable repair bill. That day, my patient Candi told me that when she arrived for her session, she saw Jean standing at the side of the house, looking at the ground. The location she described was exactly where the septic tank is located! What's astonishing is the fact that none of my patients, including Candi, knew that I was having trouble with the septic system or the location of the tank. Jean has come to Candi, who is particularly receptive to spirit, on more than one occasion. What's so striking is the fact that she never knew Jean in life nor had she seen a picture of him.

Being Aware of Our Thoughts, Feelings, Needs, and Wishes

On the night before my first birthday following Jean's departure, I gazed longingly at a bed of lilies outside a restaurant and thought, *I'll never receive flowers from you again. I would have loved a bouquet of lilies from you.* The next day, my doorbell rang. A florist was delivering a bouquet of lilies for my birthday, sent to me by my acupuncturist, Therese. She subsequently told me that she'd received a message to send me those particular flowers! Be open to the myriad ways in which spirit offers you similar signs. Remember that coincidence is spirit's way of remaining anonymous.

When Jean uses others in the service of love to give me a sign of his presence, as I said, they feel a gentle nudge to say or do something that they might not ordinarily say or do. Sometimes they will be moved to use words that aren't their own.

Again, this type of communication should not be confused with demonic possession. As I've explained, spirits choose people who are Open Vessels, who are willing to be used in the service of love.

After the fact, I usually receive confirmation that I was correct in my interpretation that Jean was borrowing an Open Vessel to speak to me. I learned this over time when these Open Vessels fail to reappear or remain in my life.

Dreams

As I said previously, when the conscious mind is asleep, our brains are more receptive to spirit.

Many people are only open enough to be contacted during dreams. The good news is that meditation enables you to access the part of the brain that is active during dream states. The more you meditate, the better you'll be at accessing this part of your psyche while you're awake.

In addition to my own dream visitation from Jean that I described earlier in the book, on more than one occasion Jean has entered my patients' dreams. The first time my patient Candi saw him was in a dream. It was when she told me this that I showed her his photo. She said, "That was the man!"

A couple of weeks later another patient, Theresa, who was going through a painful divorce, told me that a man she didn't know had vividly come to her in the middle of the night. She said that she was awakened out of a sound sleep and saw him sitting beside the bed. He had a remarkable smile and sent her the message that she would be fine. Theresa also had never met Jean or seen a photo of him. I again brought out a photo of Jean, and she said, yes, that was the man who had reassured her in the night!

Twilight States

As I discussed in the last chapter, twilight states refer to the time between waking and sleeping when our conscious mind is asleep and our superconscious mind is awake. A twilight visit feels different from a dream visitation. In this case you'll feel open and accessible to spirit, but you will be in a highly receptive state that feels like a trance. This is different from sleep.

Specters

I have heard people describe seeing specters, apparitions, mists, or other visual anomalies such as shadows or whitish images that flash across their field of vision. On more than one occasion since Jean's passing, my housekeeper and friend Donna and I have seen Jean appear to us in this fashion. I can't describe what we see any better than my patient Ruth's description of her husband, who appeared to her on the night he left his body as a whitish, wispy specter.

Candi often speaks of seeing specters. One day, her cat was behaving strangely. She photographed him, and in the photos we could see these same whitish specks that Donna and I have seen. I have heard it said that spirits vibrate at a much higher rate than humans. Perhaps these white specks are visible to the human eye only when a spirit slows down. When they vibrate at their normal speed perhaps our eyes can't perceive their energy fields.

Sounds of Spirit

Over the years, Jean has produced many inexplicable sounds, from creaking floorboards and footsteps to the door chimes that ring when my security system registers the opening of my exterior doors—but they're not being opened. A former patient of mine told me that his own doorbell chimed right after his father passed.

In addition, one evening when my massage therapist was at my house, we both heard the couch creak. The sound came from the side where Jean always sat. At the same time, the couch leg made a sliding sound, as though Jean had just sat down! Our level of scientific understanding doesn't account for such miracles. Suffice it to say, spirit beings can influence matter in ways that our technology cannot begin to explain.

Scent of Sanctity

Spirits often announce their presence by creating certain scents. On several occasions I've smelled Jean's morning toast or his favorite brand of coffee. Many people have reported a sweet smell surrounding me, even though I wasn't wearing perfume.

Another time, my friend Kris and I were dining outside on a paved patio. The traffic was whizzing past us on Route 9. In such a setting, we would have expected to smell gas fumes; instead we experienced something quite different. As I was telling Kris how important it is to keep faith alive in the darkest hours, I noticed her inhaling like a dog trying to sniff out an elusive prey. At that moment, we both smelled the sweetest perfume. The scent was similar to gardenia, jasmine, or lilies, but not exactly like any one of those. It was heavenly, unlike anything we'd ever smelled in our lives. I knew that this was a sign from Jean confirming my comment about faith.

Keeping Us Safe

Remember those in spirit often assume the role of our earthly protectors and guides. I heard a story told by a young boy whose grandfather died the week before the boy was involved in a near-fatal car accident. Just before the crash, the boy, who was sitting in the backseat, had removed his seatbelt. At the moment of impact, he felt his grandfather restraining him. Given the force of the collision, he would have gone through the windshield had it not been for his grandfather's intervention from spirit. It would seem that his grandfather left when he did because he knew that he needed to be in spirit form in order to save his grandson—again affirming that the future has already happened. Beings in spirit will use whoever is available and whatever means are needed to encourage and protect you, assist you in pursing your destiny, and support you in your journey.

Saving Our Lives

In 2010, I did a brief Internet dating stint. After a few months, I was disgusted by the various and sundry conmen who seemed to be finding me. One morning I awoke and said, "Jean, today is the day I am closing down all my profiles. Just send me a man who's real and who gets me."

I entered my office and opened up Match.com. Just as I was about to click Delete Profile, a pop-up window appeared. It invited me to migrate my profile over to Senior People Meet. I argued aloud with the screen, saying, "No, I'm swearing off Internet dating sites. Besides, I'm not a senior citizen. No!"

The next thing I knew, Jean was telling me, *Click yes!*

"No."

Click yes!

Finally I gave in.

I swear to God that one minute after my profile migrated over to the new site, I had an e-mail in my inbox from a man who wrote to me and said, "I just saw your profile. I'm real, and I get you!"

To say that I was flabbergasted is an understatement. Clearly, Jean's hand was all over this introduction!

We began chatting. Again, I had that hit-the-ground running feeling. Within six weeks, he'd arranged to come from the West Coast to where I live on the East Coast. He planned to spend a week in my area to get to know me better.

During this first visit, I showed him my house and the walk-in closet where Jean's clothing still hung. Something had always told me to not get rid of his belongings. So I hadn't.

Jean had been an unusual size. He wore a 40 regular sport coat/suit that had to be tailored to fit him. His waist size was 32, and he wore size 8 shoes and 14½ in shirts. This man tried on Jean's jacket, shoes, belts, and shirts. They fit him perfectly.

Then we went to Jean's jewelry box. Jean could wear his rings only on the left ring finger, not the right. When this man tried the ring on his right hand, he said, "This isn't a match."

I told him to try the ring on his left hand, and voilà, it fit perfectly.

One day, I leaned near him and he smelled just like Jean. Needless to say, I made the mistake of thinking that he was the clone that Jean had promised to send me. I again let my guard down.

At the end of the visit, as he was driving to the airport before sunrise, he encountered a lot of deer on the road. When he arrived back home, he said, "Promise you will never get into your Miata again. If you hit a deer in that, you'll be dead."

Since I'd never hit a deer in my life, the concern had never entered my mind. But I did say, "Okay. I promise." And I meant it.

A few weeks later, he told me that his good friend had a used Porsche to sell. He said that this car would survive a deer hit, and I went ahead and bought the vehicle. He arranged to send it to me in New York via flatbed. The delivery of the car was timed so that he would be visiting me when it arrived.

A month later, he and the Porsche were both in New York. He worked like a dog cleaning the Miata (which had been invaded by mice!) and then helped me get the Miata sold.

On this same visit, I started getting a bad feeling about this man. I discovered he was bipolar and heavily medicated. I realized that he didn't have the temperament to start a business for himself in New York—and in order to move to be closer to me, he needed a source of income.

He went home and made a date for us to watch the same movie together the following night—he on his computer, me on mine, while being on the phone. But the appointed time came and went. He didn't answer my phone call. He didn't answer my e-mail. The man literally seemed to have disappeared from the face of the earth, just as the man in Florida had. And I never heard from him again.

A couple of weeks later, my main car was in the shop, so I had to use the Porsche to drive to the group-therapy session I run on Wednesday nights. On my way home, as I was driving south at 55 miles per hour, another car was coming north. The next thing I knew, a deer leapt out from behind the northbound car. The oncoming vehicle had completely obscured the deer and it slammed into the front of my Porsche. The front of the car was smashed and the radiator began leaking.

I now realized for sure that the future has already happened. That's how Jean was able to know ahead of time that a deer would be "coming down the pike" for me. He'd sent that man to get me out of the Miata and into the Porsche in order to save my life! That's why the man disappeared as soon as the car arrived. He had served his purpose. In this case, Jean needed a human clone to protect me.

Repetition

Spirits will also use others to repeat and affirm what they've already told you, to guide you, and even to protect you. To get their point across, spirits can be nags. As I said earlier, I can't count how many times Jean has had strangers walk up to me and say, "Your husband said for you to tell your story."

Recurring Numbers, Letters, and Dates

Clues such as recurring numbers, letters, and dates are often used to inform and guide you along the path you're meant to follow. Jean left the Jesuit Order at age 48. He died when I was 48, and I entered my own spiritual ministry of sorts.

Since Jean's physical departure, I've noticed that each time I'm on the road, I see cars with the letters DGS on their license plates. Some days, no matter where I drive, I'll see ten or more different cars with these three letters. The first time I noticed it, the thought *Do God's service* popped into my mind.

Specific numbers can also be a sign of spirit presence: When visiting my New Jersey massage therapist, I heard a song about an angel being separated from his beloved by a large ocean. But the song went on to confirm that their separation wasn't forever. Jean continually kept interrupting and forcing the CD to jump back to the song about the angel. I found out afterward that this song was track 21 (the year of Jean's birth). My therapist tried three times to adjust the music, and each time she did, the CD jumped back to track 21.

Again I stress that the examples I use in this chapter are meant to portray the many diverse ways that the spirit of your loved one can manifest itself to you. No doubt there are countless other ways that you and I will experience in the years ahead. So keep your mind open and your senses ever alert to the blessings and miracle of spirit contact. Apart from the gift of your loved one in your life, knowing that your physical separation from him or her is only temporary is God's greatest gift to you.

CHAPTER 15

ESTABLISHING YOUR OWN DIALOGUE

In spirit form I am more knowing
My love for you is overflowing
I am capable of apology while I never was before
So talk with me and you will see a heart that's an open door

Dialoguing with a loved one in spirit is a conversation without beginning or end. As a babbling brook eternally flows, as the breeze murmurs through the trees, your loved ones in spirit are always whispering words of love to you. There is no beginning or end to the conversation. There is only eternity.

By now you know that spirits walk beside you, guiding you and enveloping you in an eternal embrace. Earlier, I explained how to create a state of receptivity. The eyes of your heart also know how to recognize the intricate tapestry of signs that herald spirit presence, including everything in the last chapter—inexplicable sounds and scents, odd sensations, waves of love, chills, gooseflesh, butterflies, visions and apparitions, and animals behaving oddly. Now you are on the threshold of establishing your own dialogue with a loved one in spirit form.

As you'll discover, dialoguing with spirit is poetry written on the pages of your heart. It is often wordless, and beyond time and space.

Setting the Stage

A Request Initiates the Dialogue

When you're grieving, it's easy to fall into a state of passivity—to lie down and wait to die, or to wait for your loved one to come to you. It's especially important during these times to ask for help. As you read on, you'll notice that Jean dialogues with me frequently because I ask him to. As a frail human being who misses her beloved more than words can express, I need a lot of support. I therefore ask for a lot, and I receive a lot. From this day forward never forget or be afraid to ask.

I believe there is a reason why God wants us to ask for help. In essence, the act of asking strengthens our faith. This is because when our request is fulfilled, it reaffirms the presence of God and our loved ones in spirit form. If we were to receive blessings without having asked for them, we might never think to attribute these blessings to the appropriate source.

Requesting a Dialogue Is a Form of Prayer

Jean objected to what he called utilitarian theology. He was referring to the way many people use religion like a grocery list, praying for their own personal or material gain. Jean prayed for the welfare of others. When he did pray for himself, the prayer was to inspire him to be more loving, especially to me. So beware of how you formulate your prayer. It is a humble request, not a demand, not a threat, and not a deal you're trying to close. Pray simply for the door of your heart to open so that you may be permitted to connect.

What If Nobody's Home?

Many people have told me, "I have asked, but my loved one never dialogues with me." Don't be so sure. Intense emotions can dead bolt your heart and render you blind and deaf to a spirit's attempts to communicate.

During periods of distress, I often find myself unable to receive communications from Jean. I believe that the signs of his presence are still being transmitted, but I am too upset to notice. Consider the analogy of a cell phone in a tunnel. While in the tunnel, I'm not aware that I have received a call. But as soon as I exit the tunnel, I discover a message waiting for me. Intense emotions such as grief, anger, and sadness block reception and create the illusion that we aren't receiving signals from our loved ones. It's as if an emotionally stormy climate blocks my receiver, just as atmospheric storms block the reception of television or radio signals. Jean has reminded me again and again that internal chaos interferes with my capacity for receiving messages and signs.

I believe that adverse emotional states block not only reception but also transmission. In short, my distress prevents Jean from reaching me. This may explain why messages from Jean abound when I am particularly happy and I am an Open Vessel. In fact, my openness actually seems to assist Jean in piercing the veil to reach me. Just as laughter or anger is infectious and instills a similar reaction in others, when I am more love filled and open, it seems to invite a similar reaction in Jean. His manifestations of love are then able to flow freely.

Cultivating Gratitude

At moments of distress, I also strive to cultivate gratitude, which further helps me pull out of the pit and renders me more receptive. I remind myself that many people have it much worse than I do. I use this thought to get out of my own way. I don't build myself up by stepping on someone else in misery. Rather, I focus on helping those who in fact *do* have it worse than I. Sometimes all I can do is pray for someone. In the process of praying for another, I pull myself out of my own pit.

Another way I've found to climb out of the emotional abyss is to remind myself that flowers grow even in the Sahara. I tell myself to hang on and trust that my heart will open again. And when it does, I will again be open to sharing loving communications with Jean.

Don't Push the River

Trying to force a connection is another failing proposition. I am reminded of a widowed minister who attended a talk I gave at a nursing home. We were speaking together after my presentation when her deceased husband came through to me. He told me that his wife couldn't hear him because she was trying too hard. I asked the minster if this made sense to her. She confirmed that despite the best efforts of many well-known psychic mediums, her husband had never come through to her. Likewise she had tried prayer, classic meditation, and spiritual readings; nothing had worked.

As I've been shown repeatedly, "pushing" in this manner interferes with the flow of energy. When you let go, when you surrender to the process, the energy can flow. This applies especially to contacting spirits, who are pure energy.

Please bear in mind that my discovery of how to dialogue with Jean developed over many months. Like the momentary flash of a firefly that illuminates a midnight sky, at first his words simply came to me as specks of light in the dark night of my soul. Over time, he showed me all the ways for us to dialogue. Simply follow the exercises in this book and then allow your own process to unfold.

Various Kinds of Dialogues

You're almost ready to learn my Dialoguing with the Departed technique to initiate and establish a conversation with any spirit being you choose. I remind you that even if you don't believe that spirits live on, the dialoguing process is still effective in helping you to ease your grief, heal wounds, or repair a relationship with someone who has passed over.

As you embark on dialoguing, know that you are free to decide on the nature and the extent of the relationship you wish to reestablish. The possibilities are endless. For example, if you're a parent who has lost a child or a child who has lost a parent or sibling, reconnecting and *staying* connected will likely be your goal. Likewise, if you are elderly and don't wish to form another primary relationship, reconnecting and remaining connected with your spouse will be vital to you as well.

In the event that a loved one was torn from you as a result of an accidental death or sudden illness, you were probably robbed of the chance to say a formal farewell to that person's physical being. In such cases, reconnecting will, at the very least, permit you to say good-bye.

Since your loved ones in spirit are now your guides, I encourage you to create an ongoing dialogue so that you can reach out to them to obtain guidance.

Last, but certainly not least, you can heal unfinished business and repair a damaged relationship using my dialoguing technique.

Entering a State of Receptivity

No matter your goal, before attempting to make contact with a spirit being, be sure that you are adept at entering a state of receptivity. Also be sure that you're able to recognize the signs of spirit presence. Only when you are open and can see such signs are you ready to dialogue. Just as you would never think of engaging in a phone conversation if no one is on the other end of the line, don't try to dialogue with a spirit before you feel that being's presence.

If you attempt to dialogue before you've cultivated your ability to be open to spirit, you will feel utterly frustrated and even bereft. So be patient and remember that fine wine takes time. And don't forget that you have all the time in the world. Spirit beings have no perception of time as we understand it, and they aren't going anywhere! They're ready when you are.

Dialoguing with the Departed

It is vital to keep in mind that dialoguing with a spirit being isn't akin to the verbal communications we share with one in bodily form. Because a spirit is freed from the human vessel, that being can dialogue with you in unearthly ways that extend far beyond simple back-and-forth verbal discussions. So don't ever expect to dialogue in a strictly verbal sense. While it's true that some people are clairaudient, meaning that they can audibly hear the voice of a spirit being, most likely you won't be hearing a voice and carrying on conversations the same way you do with those in human bodies.

Mind Melding

The above notwithstanding, you can still verbally dialogue with a spirit being through a process known as "mind melding." This occurs when a spirit implants words or thoughts into your mind. The message is communicated not by an actual audible voice but rather by words, images, thoughts, or notions that you know are not your own suddenly popping into your head. They have come from elsewhere, seemingly out of nowhere. Because spirits are pure energy, their thoughts can enter our minds unimpeded. All human beings have the innate capacity to send and receive brain waves, which enables us to communicate telepathically. Our capacity to do this seems positively correlated to the degree of emotional connection we have with someone. For example, we've all heard stories of twins who perceive a silent call from the other who is in trouble, of members of close married couples who often know what their partner is thinking, and of mothers who describe a telepathic link to their children.

Mind melding is a form of clairsentience in which we're able to receive or sense the thoughts of a loved one in spirit form. As I stated previously, when a spirit communicates with you via clairsentience, it's not like being hit by a Mack truck. It's a subtle experience. So remember, when a thought that you know isn't your own suddenly pops into your head, be open to the possibility that it's a message from spirit.

As you become more comfortable with recognizing when mind melding occurs, and "hearing" spirit, you can then go a step further and engage in a fluid back-and-forth dialogue.

You do this by making a statement and then allowing yourself to sit utterly still. In the quiet that follows, you may "hear" a word, a sentence, or many sentences in response. Then it's your turn to respond and be still and allow spirit to insert the next word, series of words, or images into your mind. By continuing in this way, you can achieve a back-and-forth dialogue.

You may find it easier to engage in the dialogue silently or you may choose to speak aloud, saying both your own thoughts and then speaking spirit's response. Choose whatever feels most natural for you.

Dialoguing in Writing

You can also engage in a back-and-forth dialogue using the automatic writing technique I mentioned in Chapter 5. The best time to engage in automatic writing is when the heart is bursting with pain. So, don't try to schedule a time or place. Just listen to your heart.

When you sit down with pen and paper, don't worry about reason or conscious thought—just write. The process feels similar to free-associating. Soon, you may find your loved one guiding your pen. Let the process flow, welcoming spirit's words and en-gaging in dialogue as it feels appropriate.

If writing doesn't come naturally to you, it's also possible to speak aloud and record your conversations with a loved one in spirit. You can use a manually operated or voice-activated recorder that you keep on your person, and just speak aloud whenever your heart begins to well up with pain. Then audibly speak spirit's responses as they come to you.

Dialoguing Exercise

While sitting or lying down, close your eyes and inhale deeply through your mouth. Hold your breath for a count of five, then exhale through mouth. Repeat this cycle ten times.

Next, repeat the Visualization to Enter a Trance meditation from Chapter 13. Be sure that you've released all tension from your body before moving on to the next step.

When you're fully relaxed and receptive, imagine yourself strolling along the bank of a stream. The sky is a perfect blue dome, a gentle breeze ruffles the lush grass, and songbirds and butterflies accompany your stroll.

As you walk on, your steps become lighter until they are nearly weightless.

A stream meanders lazily in front of you. You effortlessly cross the stream and enter a meadow that is an emerald carpet.

As you walk, you see a large lake in the distance. Its surface is smooth as glass and shimmers like liquid silver.

The lake seems to have a magnetic force that pulls you toward it. As you approach, you notice your loved one standing at the edge of the lake, smiling and beckoning you forward. His or her eyes sparkle as he or she stretches his or her arms out to you in welcome. Your loved one sends you the message energetically that it is time for you to open your heart and speak the words that your heart begs you to share.

If you merely wish to reconnect, the dialoguing that follows will be a straightforward reestablishment of communication. Speak aloud, take notes of what you say and what you hear, or tape the sessions. Record your words as well as the words you hear in response.

Should you need to heal your relationship and repair Old Scars, the dialoguing process is a bit more complicated. Begin by talking aloud about whatever emotional burden still troubles your heart. Say everything that you've held back, everything that you've never had the nerve or opportunity to utter. Write as you speak, or tape the dialogue. Again, make sure to record not only what you say, but also what you hear.

Continue this back-and-forth discussion for as long as you wish. Each time you wish to continue your dialogue, repeat the visualization and preparation process and pick up your conversation where you left off. Keep a written or audio journal as a record of the progress you're making.

Conducting a Group Séance

When engaging in a dialogue in my office during an individual or group setting, I begin by allowing a spirit to speak through me. Initially I act as a sort of spiritual training wheels, a medium or spokesperson who speaks on behalf of the being in spirit. I do this until my patient has learned how to "coast" on his or her own and engage in an unassisted conversation.

You might like to try hosting a séance with a group of like-minded friends in which you work together to facilitate the dialoguing process. If one of the members of the group is more advanced in the process of connecting with spirit, he or she can facilitate the group. If no one in your intimate circle is more skilled than another, that's all right. Practice the exercises I outline and cultivate your skills together. In much the same way that people find it easier to enter a meditative trance when they're working in a group setting, because brain waves seem to be infectious, you'll also find it easier to develop your skills if you work in a group with other people who wish to cultivate their ability to communicate with spirit.

A group can consist of two or more people. Ideally, you don't want to have more than eight people. The larger the group, the less intimate and the more intimidating the experience can be.

To facilitate trust, it helps to have a group composed of the same members from one session to the next. This way, you will come to know one another's stories, which helps develop a sense of safety and trust. Of course, if a newly grieving person wishes to join, open your arms to that person. Remember what Jean said: *We're all one family. We're all one religion. That religion is love.* So open your arms in love to anyone who wishes to participate. You will find yourself united in grief even with total strangers.

To develop your skills, approach the process with discipline. Meet at a regular time each week. Choose a setting in which you won't be overheard or disturbed by phones or children.

Above all, when it comes to dialoguing with spirit, don't be governed by rules. Just do what feels right for the group as a whole and make sure that every member takes a part of the time, if he or she wishes.

If everyone agrees, you can ask each person to take a turn in leading the group. Follow the progression that I outline in this book, starting with cultivating your receptivity, and then moving into dialoguing when the group feels ready. If some members don't feel skilled enough to dialogue yet, that's all right, too. In my experience, group members learn and heal simply by witnessing other dialogues.

Again, remind yourself that as we learn to walk, we need to be propped up until we can stand on our own. Similarly, we all need training wheels until we can learn to dialogue on our own. Soon enough, you will be able to cast off the training wheels and carry on your own unassisted conversation.

Obstacles to Dialoguing with the Departed

If you find that you're having difficulty establishing a dialogue, don't despair. When you first attempt it, you may need a little assistance. I have a dear friend who, before becoming a Catholic priest later in life, was a married man who lost his beloved wife in a tragic car accident. He's a deeply spiritual man who's open to the concept of communicating with spirits, and he was immersed in prayer, meditation, and spiritual readings. Despite this, he found himself unable to communicate with his wife's spirit for several years, even though he felt her spirit residing within him.

I was especially traumatized by my early birth and a lifetime of sickness and emotional pain, all of which enabled me to be especially open to spirit communications. Because you likely haven't shared my unusual experiences, you may need a little more effort to access this skill that lies dormant within each of us.

I'm reminded of Jan, a former group-therapy patient of mine whom I'll discuss in greater length later in this chapter. The first time her father communicated with her, I literally spoke on his behalf. But the second time we attempted to dialogue, she heard a partial sentence. Another group member heard her father's entire sentence at the same moment I did. It wasn't long before Jan was capable of engaging in her own dialogues with her dad. With time and effort, you, like Jan, will find yourself increasingly skilled in dialoguing with spirit.

Lingering Fear of an Abusive Parent

Even though you now know intellectually that beings are more knowing and seeing in the spirit realm than they were here on earth, as well as more capable of love and forgiveness, and even though you know it's possible to heal issues that couldn't have been resolved during the spirit being's lifetime, you still may feel doubtful or resistant to trying.

I've noticed that many of my clients who were abused by a parent or other relative when they were young continue to feel afraid to dialogue with that being in spirit, for fear of being abused again. Although we realize that the feeling is irrational, it often hangs on regardless.

If this is your fear, you need to be reminded that spirit beings are more evolved. Through this elevated perspective, spirits are more able to relinquish their less desirable traits and fine-tune their better ones. (As I stated in the previous chapter, because spirit beings are more evolved than when they lived in a physical state, it even may be necessary to wait until a person passes in order to heal any unresolved issues that still linger. Therefore, I ask you to never give up the hope of healing a relationship with someone who has passed.)

Sometimes knowing that spirit beings are evolved helps a person feel more confident about trying to dialogue with them. But sometimes it does not. Why?

Initially, many of my patients feel that it's impossible to make amends with a parent who is deceased. Such expressions of futility stem from our early memories of the damaged and scary parent of our youth. If this is the case for you, I encourage you to remind yourself that you're grown up now and not a child anymore. And the person who abused you isn't the same being in spirit form. They are now ready, willing, able, and patiently waiting (maybe that's what waiting an eternity really means!) to work it out with you and bring you peace of mind.

Despite these affirmations, you may still feel scared that you'll be beaten or punished for speaking out of line, especially if you never had the chance to confront your abuser and clear the air when he or she still lived in a body. No matter how old you are chronologically, if you haven't worked through the emotions associated with the abuse you suffered when you were young, the abused child of your youth will continue to live on inside of you. Like every other abused person, you will remain emotionally frozen in time, as scared of that parent as when you were young. You will continue to feel this way long after your parent is dead—time will not diminish the fear.

Helping Spirits Evolve

On my first Good Friday following Jean's passing, I felt led to visit a woman named Laurie who sells exotic birds. I hadn't spoken to her or seen her in five years, since we put Fluffy, our beloved canary, to sleep. I knew nothing of her personal life.

As I approached her house, I felt that I'd been sent to help her and one of her birds. As soon as I walked inside, she showed me a young female finch that was dying. She explained that finches can't go more than a day without food, and this little one hadn't eaten for a day. Laurie said that she wouldn't last much longer.

The bird sat motionless on the perch. Her feathers were puffed up.

I asked Laurie if I could try to heal the bird and she agreed, so I walked over to the birdcage and pressed my face to the thin metal bars. Normally having someone come this close would distress a bird. This creature was not distressed.

As I began talking to the bird, she became aware of my presence and then became excited. She started jumping up and down and even began flying!

I told her aloud that I wanted her to go to her seed bowl and begin eating. The bird obeyed me immediately. The more that she ate, the stronger she became and the more she wanted to eat. By this point, she was scarfing up seeds like a miniature vacuum cleaner.

It was then that I felt a tidal wave of love and realized that it was Jean who had led me here. In this elegantly orchestrated manifestation, he was simultaneously blessing Laurie by allowing me to save her bird, and also giving me the blessing of saving her little bird the way I couldn't save Fluffy.

I then sensed two spirit presences surrounding Laurie. I picked up an extreme sense of urgency, as though they were beating down my door in their eagerness to speak to her. I also had the sense that they'd been waiting for a long time to reach her and that they were relieved that I'd heard the call and was there to help them talk to her.

At that moment, I saw that the bird had sensed their presence as well. She looked distressed again and had started stretching her head heavenward. It occurred to me that the spirit presences surrounding Laurie may have been upsetting the little creature and may have caused her sickness.

I told the bird aloud not to worry about these spirits. While speaking aloud may make it easier for me to transmit a clear energetic message, I've also silently communicated a message to animals and they have understood me all the same. In this case, I spoke aloud because I wanted Laurie to hear what I was saying. I was here to help Laurie with the spirits, and the bird should return to her meal. She did!

I then heard a female spirit presence say to Laurie, *I am so sorry that I was such a weakling and didn't protect you.* When I repeated the word *weakling* to Laurie, it struck me as an odd term, certainly not one that I would ever use.

I sensed that it was Laurie's mother speaking, but I didn't know that she was dead.

I asked Laurie if these words made sense to her. She said that they did and confirmed that, indeed, it was her mother speaking. She added that her mother always used the word *weakling*. I've come to realize that not only Jean but also other spirits validate their presence by using figures of speech that were idiosyncratic to them.

I then heard her mother expanding on her previous message. She said, *I'm sorry that I couldn't protect you from your father.*

Laurie again confirmed that this was true.

At that moment I felt a man desperately trying to reach out to Laurie. I said, "There's a man who wants to speak to you. He wants you to know you're safe. He can't hurt you anymore."

As I said that, I felt my eyes being drawn to a cranberry-colored blown-glass ball hanging from the ceiling. I was momentarily confused since I'd purchased an identical item as a gift for someone around five years before, but in that moment I couldn't recall to whom I'd given it. I asked Laurie if I'd given the ornament to her. She said no, that she'd bought the "witching" ball to protect her from the spirit of her father. I then realized that her father had drawn my attention to the ball as a way to get her to talk about her ongoing emotions.

"I am still afraid of him," Laurie told me.

Her father replied, *I'm not asking you to forgive me. For your own sake as well as mine, all I ask is that you confront me. Now is the time to make me face up to what I did to you. Don't protect me. You need this for your own healing. And I need you to help me face the truth in order for me to evolve spiritually.*

This experience was a first for me and it utterly amazed me. I had discovered that, in order to progress spiritually, those who have passed over actually need us to help them in their evolution!

Here's the beauty of this process. As we help those in spirit to evolve, we're helping ourselves. As this example shows, Laurie remained frozen in time, trapped in childhood, because the feelings associated with the trauma she suffered as a child hadn't been resolved. So she continued to drown in the terror of a young girl who doesn't feel safe. Dialoguing with her father, through me, was just what she needed to help them both heal and evolve. By the time I left that day, Laurie was already standing taller and felt less afraid of her father. And her little bird made it, too!

Supervised Visitations

To further overcome the fear of dialoguing, I find it's helpful to visualize the adult part of your psyche presiding over the dialogue and protecting your frightened inner child. I call this a "supervised visitation." By watching over the encounter, you are truly re-parenting yourself, helping the little person inside you to speak to the parent who harmed you and assuring the little one that you're there to protect him or her. Now is your chance to say what's been nagging at your heart, knowing that you, the adult, will be watching over you as you speak to your parent or other family member who harmed you.

In addition, I have found that it helps my patients when we "defang" or disempower their parents or other abusers before initiating a dialogue. Use whatever image works for you. Some prefer to visualize the spirit of the parent sitting across the room from them strapped into a chair, to further remove the fear of being physically harmed by the parent. If you're afraid of being verbally assailed, then by all means stuff an imaginary sock into your parent's mouth. Create whatever visualization you need in order to feel safe.

Anger as an Impediment to Dialoguing

Not wanting to let go of resentment can create another obstacle to dialoguing with a spirit being. I remind you that if you're carrying resentment toward someone who has mistreated or abused you, you aren't expected to force forgiveness on yourself. Beings in spirit accept you as you are, right where you are. You can be angry; you can rage at them for as long as you need to. They have an eternity to work it out with you, and as I've stated, they aren't going anywhere! All you need to do is open your emotional door and begin the process of sharing the feelings in your heart. Share your hurt. Share your anger. Let the spirit simply listen and understand you. Just start talking and allow the process of healing to begin. What spirit beings want is for you to allow them to right their wrongs, to make peace with you, and to shower you with love. And they're eager to get started!

For example, a lapsed Catholic woman came to see me because of the relentless grief she experienced after the accidental death of her daughter. The woman told me that she was furious with her daughter for dying. As irrational as it may seem, anger is a common reaction to being left behind by a loved one. She also told me that as a result of her daughter's death, she had lost her faith in God and no longer believed in the afterlife.

Within minutes, I had the sensation of her daughter pounding on my psychic door, desperately trying to get through to me. She showed me a perfect set of white teeth and I asked her mother why. The mother told me that in life her daughter had been ashamed of her crooked dark teeth. So clearly the daughter wanted her mother to know that her flaws were now gone!

You'd have thought that this remarkable manifestation would have cooled her mother's anger and melted her heart. But it did neither.

The next week, during a second session, this woman's daughter tried a different approach. She told me, *Ask my mother about Padre Pio,* and so I did. According to reports, Padre Pio is the first stigmatized priest in the history of the Church, receiving visible marks of the crucifixion when he knelt in front of a large crucifix.

To my utter stupefaction, the mother jumped off the couch and shouted at me, "Why did you say Padre Pio?"

"Because your daughter asked me to," I told her.

The mother burst into tears. The mother told me that Padre Pio was her daughter's favorite saint. The girl talked about him daily. By asking me to provide this detail to her mother, she was powerfully proving her presence.

The mother said through her tears, "I feel my daughter now. I feel her right here beside me."

In this case, confirmation of her daughter's presence dissolved the anger that was impeding their dialogue. From then on she was able to conduct her own direct dialogue. Her anger and grief rapidly subsided, and she concluded therapy soon afterward. Bad for business but good for her!

Playing the Victim

A patient of mine named Louise had been holding on her entire life to what she referred to as a boatload of anger toward her mother. Each time I encouraged her to dialogue with her mother in spirit, she resisted because she clearly had no desire to make peace. She was welded to her anger. While a strict religious upbringing may have been partially responsible for her resistance to expressing anger at her parents, it was not the real reason she remained stuck with her rage.

In reality, Louise's anger sounded more like the complaints of a victim stuck in a vacuum. She would rail on like a broken record, detailing again and again the same old stories about how wronged, mistreated, and neglected she'd been as a child. Her story is not unique. Many children learn to play the role of victim because they weren't allowed to voice their anger during childhood. This causes the anger to go underground and then resurface in the form of self-victimization. Each time we bemoan our miserable state, we're unconsciously venting anger. The victim points the finger and indirectly blames the abuser by saying, "Look how you hurt me and ruined my life!"

I had another patient who told me that when she was young, she used to run full speed into a wall to knock herself unconscious. Just before she blacked out, she would think, *My parents are really going to suffer once they realize how much they've hurt me.* Suicide is the ultimate expression of this way of thinking and reacting. The person committing suicide will often fantasize that he or she is punishing the living through his or her death.

To return to Louise, I realized that in order for her to be set free of her victimized attitude, which was preventing her from dialoguing with her mother, she needed to understand her mother. I created the following exercise to help her do this. If you're holding on to anger and feel unable to dialogue as a result, I encourage you to try this exercise.

Being a Spirit's Spokesperson Exercise

I had Louise use the Dialoguing Exercise presented earlier in this chapter. Then, when she met her mother, I asked her to imagine that her mother was actually stepping inside her.

Next, I asked Louise to allow her mother to speak from her heart and to tell Louise everything that she felt about her own life, about her daughter, and about her marriage to Louise's father.

Words began pouring out and Louise wept as she spoke. When she emerged from this exercise, she was a changed woman. Prior to this moment, she'd never understood the harsh realities of her mother's life. Allowing her mother to enter her and speak brought about an epiphany of understanding. For the first time in Louise's life, she felt true empathy for her mother's struggles and challenges. In that sublime moment, I watched a lifetime of anger dissipate before my eyes and a new relationship between mother and daughter take root. The moral of this story, of course, is that it's never too late to establish a loving relationship with a being in spirit.

Guilt as an Obstacle to Dialoguing

One day as I was walking down 47th Street, which is the jewelry district of New York City, I felt drawn to enter a specific building. I was then led to a particular display booth where I felt urged to tell the story of my life with Jean in spirit form. In no time at all, the owner of the store and her assistant were in tears. The owner's best friend had lost her beloved husband of 30 years just a couple of years previously, and she was having a hard time working through the grieving process. She'd gone to see a grief therapist as well as a psychiatrist. Despite being put on medications, she remained depressed with not much will to live.

As I heard this, I felt a chill running up my spine accompanied by an intense sense of urgency. This woman's husband was desperately trying to reach his wife, through me, with this message: *Tell her that she's not hearing me because she's too upset to hear me.* I asked the owner to have her friend, whose name was Ginny, give me a call at her convenience.

Three weeks later she did. As soon as I heard Ginny's voice, I felt her husband's presence and felt the same chills over my body. The first thing she told me, once we'd done away with formalities and gotten down to business, was that although she'd been desperate to connect with her husband, Bob, he hadn't come to her even in dreams.

"He doesn't have to," I said. "He's with you all the time."

I told her that her depth of grief was rendering her deaf to him, and she said that she had the sense that this was true. I explained that her lack of familiarity with signs of spirit presence could also be making her blind to his being there with her. I began rattling off examples of signs and, sure enough, she said that she'd experienced many of the phenomena I described. She told me, for example, that the day after her husband died, all the lights blew out in the house. She thought that was weird since there had been no storms or power outages in the neighborhood. I told her that spirits are pure energy, and as such often affect the operation of electronic equipment.

Then she told me that Bob's favorite watch had a battery that needed to be changed every few months. "That watch just keeps right on ticking," she said, "even though I haven't changed the battery in years."

"The battery in Bob's watch isn't dead," I assured her, "because Bob isn't dead. That's his message to you."

In no time, I felt his love for her surrounding me, just as I felt the well of tears in my eyes. I heard him say, *Tell her that I'm holding her hand every minute.* When I asked her if he'd held her hand in life, she said, "Every minute."

Then I heard Bob say that Ginny shouldn't blame herself for refusing to allow them to perform the operation.

I asked her what that meant, and she confessed to me that she'd been blaming herself for not consenting to an operation that could have prolonged Bob's life. I realized then that it was her guilt that had been blocking her from reconnecting and dialoguing with her husband.

Bob told her, through me, that she needed to accept that it was simply his time and that it was no one's fault. He also said that starting that night he wanted her to sleep on his shoulder again.

I asked her if that is how they used to sleep, and she said yes, it was.

Then he said, *Ginny, take heart.*

When I asked her if these words were meaningful to her, she nodded, and I could hear her holding back tears. She told me that she's a songwriter and her trademark is writing songs with the word *heart* in them!

Needless to say, our experience lifted her heart and mine—as I hope it lifts yours.

Sexual Abuse as an Obstacle to Dialoguing

Jan, whom I mentioned earlier in this chapter, is a woman whose father left home when she was eight. He never again made contact with her. Since the day he left, Jan lived in a state of constant fear. Decades ago, following a hysterectomy, she had a mental breakdown and was hospitalized. She took all kinds of prescription drugs and still suffered from constant panic attacks.

One day in April, she fell into an even deeper depression. The year before, she and I had determined why her worst states of depression occurred in the month of April. That was because her father had left in April.

One evening during a group session she said, "I thought that once we figured that out, I wouldn't be depressed anymore."

I shook my head. "But you haven't *talked* to him and told him about how you feel about his leaving," I explained. "For the depression to ease, you need to reconnect with him and tell him how you feel about his abandoning you."

She said she didn't know where to start. But then she closed her eyes and the words started pouring out: "How could you have walked away, never to contact me again? I went to the mailbox every day of my life hoping to hear from you. You broke my heart, and for that I hate you. How can I love you and hate you at the same time?"

She went on that way for 15 minutes, after which I asked her if she'd like to have her father join the conversation. Did she want him to respond?

She said, "Yes, if it's really him."

She then heard him say, *I didn't know what else to do.* She heard this in her head at the same moment that the thought was implanted in my mind. He continued, *I knew my behavior was wrong and I didn't know what else to do but run away.*

"Yes," she responded, "and for that I hate you."

I can't rest until I know you are at peace.

"I'll never be at peace," she responded. "You can't make this up to me. You can't get off that easily. I truly do hate you."

You can be mad at me for as long as you need to be . . . for eternity if need be. I'm holding you while you kick and punch me. My arms are around you, and you have to know you're safe. I won't ever violate you again.

Jan said, "I needed your love then, when I was a child. But you left me. And now you're too late."

We don't know how you will feel, he said. *I know you will feel better and less burdened if you tell me everything. I'm not asking you to forgive me or not to be mad at me. Just speak your heart.*

"Why did you do it?" she barked at him. "Why did you just walk away from me forever? How *could* you?"

I was ashamed about what I had done to you, he replied. *I had abused you sexually, and I could never forgive myself for doing that. The only way that I could live with the guilt was to pull the plug and pretend you didn't exist. That way I could pretend that I hadn't done anything wrong. What I did to you was terrible. It was sinful, and my decision to leave you was just as bad. I have regretted it ever since. Now I can't rest until I know that I've helped you to heal. I want you to know that you never did anything wrong. You weren't responsible for my bad behavior and you weren't responsible for my leaving.* He paused, then continued, *But since my death, I have been with you all the time. I never went anywhere. I was just waiting for you to come to me.*

I then heard him say, *Now is the time to start your journal.*

When I asked Jan if she was thinking of writing a journal, she allowed that she was: "Last night I took one out, but I couldn't begin. I didn't know how to."

The following week Jan returned to my office and told me that she was at last finding a semblance of peace. It wouldn't be an easy road for her, but with further dialoguing with her father and writing in her journal, perhaps she could come to grips with what had happened and fashion a new life for herself, one without fear and one that helps children of abusive parents. In time, she said, she wanted to become a foster parent and perhaps open a safe house for abused kids. And perhaps, in greater time, even reconcile with her father.

I wished her every success in the world.

If you have endured the horror of being sexually abused, I encourage you to begin the process of healing your pain through dialoguing. Even if you are writing, speak *aloud a*nd say whatever you feel without censoring yourself. Allow yourself to feel your rage and *voice* your anger for as long as you feel the need to do so. Speaking aloud is particularly healing in these cases, as you're correcting for the silence of childhood and all the years that you didn't put voice to your outrage. When you speak, accept yourself where you are. As you continue the dialoguing, allow yourself to be open to your feelings evolving. This is your path to emotional healing.

Dialoguing When You Don't Believe

Pete's dad died when he was two and a half years old. His mother went to pieces. He was afraid that if she continued to fall apart, he would be left completely alone, left to die. From then on he walled off his feelings, so as to not further burden his mother. As an adult, he was closed off, unable to cry, unable to experience deep love, unable to trust anyone, unable to marry.

In a group-therapy session, another man began speaking about a bill he was advocating. He described in detail the purpose of the bill and asked the group members to go online and support it. Pete became argumentative, asking more and more questions to try to determine the true purpose of the bill. He said to the man, "I want to understand why my first reaction is not to believe what you're telling me, even though I realize you're trustworthy."

Pete then told a story about the day his dad died. Not knowing that his father was gone, he placed his dad's slippers in front of his red chair that night, and kept doing so night after night. It was an emotional story, but in the telling, Pete made a joke that he would write a song about it, showing the group that he was detached from his own emotional experience.

Other group members were moved to tears. Someone said, "I bet no one gave you the straight story about what happened to your dad." Another said, "Maybe you kept asking questions to try to make sense of what you were being told. Maybe now when you don't like the answer or you don't understand the answer you're receiving, you just keep asking until you hear the answer you want."

I said it would be good for him to talk to his deceased mother about what had happened. Since Pete didn't believe in God or the afterlife, I said to him, "Let's imagine you returning to your childhood. Talk to me. Tell me what you see when you think of that time in your life."

Even though Pete himself didn't believe in the afterlife, I am sure that the group felt that his mom was indeed visiting him and helping him create a healing reconstruction of his childhood.

He said that he saw his mother crying. He said that he was frozen in fear and couldn't move. I asked him if he could imagine my taking the little boy's hand so that we could go together to talk with his mom. He said he'd rather we take his inner child out to play. I offered, "We have enough people here to make up a softball team. Shall we do that?"

He nodded and said, "Yes, but I'd like one group member to stay back and watch over my mom." After a minute, he said he wanted to check in and see how his mom was doing. I pretended to contact the group member who was watching her. He said that Pete's mom was fine.

Hearing that, Pete said he wanted to return to her. I asked if the group could come with him, so that the young Pete wouldn't feel alone when speaking to his mother.

He agreed. Then the most astonishing thing happened. Pete, who always refused to cry, burst into tears and said, "I want mom to know that I'm so very grateful that she didn't abandon me."

This burst of emotion was a breakthrough since he had been walling off his emotions to protect his mother ever since he was a young boy.

Feeling his mother's presence move through me, I spoke on her behalf. I knew that from Pete's point of view, this was simply a therapeutic role-play exercise. I said, "I appreciate your gratitude. Now I want you to do one more thing for me. Stop protecting me from your feelings. I don't need this protection anymore. I want you to allow yourself to feel and to grieve, to come back to life and live it fully."

Pete did as his mother bade him, and from that moment his life and relationships both inside and outside the group were more alive and joyful than ever before.

Now you have a brief overview of how my Dialoguing with the Departed technique can be used to reconnect in order to heal grief, to re-establish and heal a relationship, and even to maintain an ongoing bond.

I urge you to begin your own process of dialoguing so that you may heal any unfinished business that continues to burden your heart. It's time to transform your grief to joy.

CHAPTER 16

SEEKING THE OASIS OF LOVE

I crawl through the desert of despair
I thought I saw an oasis
It was only a mirage

No matter what religion you do or don't profess, what culture you're from, whether you're gay or straight, young or old, male or female, whether you realize it or not, you, like all humans, are in a lifelong search for peace and love. Granted, some people who have been burned by life may wall themselves off from love, choosing to dwell within the popular fortress known as "sour grapes." Their protests, however delivered, are nothing more than a revolt against the universal need to love and to be loved.

Peace and love are like conjoined twins, bound together by shared vital organs. One twin can't survive without the other. Unfortunately, most Westerners travel a frenzied path that will never lead to peace or love.

Imagine our existence as a quest to find an oasis in the desert. Most of us believe this respite consists of an abundance of material wealth and possessions, which we hope will fill the void that dwells within us. So we live our lives in overdrive, chasing after this dream, panting as we race along the fast track. We're perpetually stressed out, buried in work, and up to our necks in obligations. We eat fast food on the run. We send a text message here and an e-mail there, and revert to social media to inform us and keep us close to presumed "friends," most of whom care hardly a fig for us. Like rats on a wheel, we seem to be forever running in place and getting nowhere, rarely pausing long enough to catch our breath.

Not knowing another path to take, we quest ahead, hoping to finally reach the oasis that we believe will quench our souls that are dying of thirst. Perhaps we attempt to fill the hollow pit with sex, drugs, food, excess work, or whatever other addictive activity temporarily puts our souls to sleep and dulls the pain. After a brief rest at the watering hole of our favorite addiction, we continue traveling the road that we believe will lead us to the oasis.

As we journey on this path, we may have sampled a few sips of material comfort and success. Having deluded ourselves into believing that money and material possessions will finally bring us the peace our souls crave, when we continue to feel discontent and empty, we simply assume that we haven't achieved *enough* of what we're after. Blinded by our illusions, we just raise the bar, set loftier goals, and work ever harder.

The Mirage

But no matter how much we acquire, no matter how much success we achieve, we are still not happy, nor are we at peace. This is because no amount of worldly success or material possessions can possibly fill the gaping void within. It will never bring peace of mind, body, and spirit to the spiritually bankrupt soul.

We find ourselves utterly lost in the desert, gasping in front of what we thought was our salvation, but which is, in fact, a mirage. Now we are dying of thirst—which keeps us searching after the only respite we know. Yet each time we think we've found the oasis, our hopes are once again dashed as we face an empty mirage.

By this point we are beaten, broken, and in despair. Our spiritual reserves have run dry.

If the struggle hasn't done us in completely, if we're lucky enough to awaken, we open our eyes, as I did, and see that the oasis was in front of us all along. It is only when we surrender our obsessive chase after the mirage of material possessions that we can discover the true oasis.

The True Oasis of Love

It's often when life has beaten us down sufficiently—when our bodies are battered by emotional or physical trauma, when our hearts have been torn open by loss, when we are too tired and demoralized to push on, when all the walls have dissolved—that we discover we've finally arrived at the oasis. To drink at the oasis is to love all those who cross our path.

But to drink we must be in the now. Living in the present is the only way to touch the endless love of spirit. For spirit doesn't live in the past or future. As we connect to others in the moment, we are engaged in the ultimate act of worship: Relationships are religion. Connection is our chapel.

As we allow ourselves to drink from the oasis of love, we discover a heart that is an overflowing well. Each time our well delivers water, each time we pour love onto others, our well is filled anew. Loving others, emotionally connecting to others, is the truest source of our energy and of our peace.

Notice I said we must love others. I did not say that others must love us in return. When we give love, it is returned to us in abundance. But we must beware of giving with the hidden agenda of receiving. If we do this, we are engaged in a variant of utilitarian religion, which is the opposite of true spirituality. Our oasis is loving others without expectation.

Surrender the Illusion of Control

It is the illusion of control that prevents us from obtaining the oasis of peace and love that we seek. It leads us down the wrong path and drives us farther and farther away from the oasis.

The first crack in the armor of my own illusion of control occurred when I discovered that many of the major events of Jean's life happened on the same month and day. As I said, on September 17, newspapers worldwide announced that Jean had left the Jesuit Order and the priesthood. His father died before having read the paper on that very same morning. Decades later, Jean wrote me a love letter on September 17, saying that he was free from the chains of his loveless and unconsummated marriage and could now spend the rest of his life with me. And Jean left his body on September 17! I've encountered numerous similar examples, which have shown me that there are no coincidences.

As I commented earlier, what appears to be coincidence is spirit's way of remaining anonymous. When I realized that major events of Jean's life did not occur at random, I found it easier to surrender the illusion of control, to accept that there are forces larger than myself guiding my fate.

Of course, nothing lasts forever. The stresses of life constantly conspire to turn light into dark and knock us off our spiritual tower. Each time we fall prey to fear, we are being taught a vital spiritual lesson. As I discovered, fear is the opposite of faith.

Live in the Present, Live in Love

My experience has shown me that it is only by living in the perfect present that each of us can finally see our true path in life, which is to love others. Interestingly, self-love is the precondition for this. We cannot give to others what we're unable to offer ourselves. So as we learn to embrace ourselves in love, we're simultaneously perfecting our ability to love those who walk the earth.

And as we unlock the door of our heart, we discover that love is the key that unlocks the door to spirit, for love is the only currency of connection (or should I say "current" of connection) to the spirit realm.

Now, I am not saying that we should live out of a cardboard box, sing "All You Need Is Love," and eat bonbons all day. Of course we're all supposed to do our best to benefit others and contribute to society. Then, after we have given our best efforts and our finest visualizations and affirmations, we must let go, surrender all expectations, turn our palms up, and detach ourselves from whatever may be the outcome, remembering it is "thy will, not my will."

As I close this chapter, I pray that you will allow the hamster wheel of frenetic activity to finally stop spinning. For it is only when you stop pushing and simply allow yourself to "be" that you will experience the internal stillness and peace of mind in the perfect present, where you may find the overflowing and boundless love of spirit.

AFTERWORD

I was driving recently on a country lane, en route to a therapy group I lead. Out of the mist, a young doe appeared, standing motionless in front of my car in the middle of the road. I wondered why the deer hadn't gotten out of the way.

Then I noticed that her left front leg was injured. She wasn't able to bear weight on it. As she began struggling to finish limping her way across, I felt a stabbing pain in my heart and tears welling in my eyes.

The poor creature finally made it to the other side of the road. I opened my window and spoke lovingly to her, tears streaming down my cheeks. I asked aloud, "Who will take care of you? It's so cold, and you have no warm place to lie down, to rest and heal."

I told her that I was so sorry that she was suffering and I wished I could help her. All I could do is what I did: send her a wave of love.

Time stood still. The deer stared into my eyes and listened to me. I stared back into her chocolate-brown eyes and noted the moonlight shimmering on her velvety coat. We were two loving beings, connected by the kinship of all life. It was at once both a painful and beautiful moment . . . and it was then I realized the lesson I was learning.

Life is full of pain and suffering. Our purpose isn't to avoid that. We aren't supposed to sidestep the aches that tear at our hearts, the rage that makes our limbs tremble, the fear that sheens our skin in the dead of night. Our purpose is to face our feelings and fully connect to others in our pain and in theirs. Life is a death sentence for most of us, not because of what we feel, but because of what we *don't* allow ourselves to feel: hate, fear, anger, love, passion, and jealousy. We avoid such emotions because we think we can't survive them. But feelings don't kill us; subverting them does. So we live a walking death, a life sentence that ends with regret over never having fully lived.

In writing this, I'm reminded of a patient who came to me because she couldn't have an orgasm. I soon realized that she was under the influence of psychological anesthesia. She had put her psyche to sleep because she was afraid to experience her feelings of anger. When we anesthetize or suppress negative emotions, we end up unable to feel pleasure and joy. We are unable to hold others dear when we're emotionally frozen in the headlights of our fear.

So often our lives are reduced to nothing more than a psychological chess game. Like icy marble chess pieces, we withdraw, retreat, and sidestep feelings, or engage in defensive tactics fueled by fear that a past trauma will follow us into the future. We imagine nightmarish "what if" scenarios of how we might be hurt all over again. In doing this, we become alienated from ourselves and from others, never fully engaged in our own lives. We die a slow death, trapped in emotional coffins of our own making.

Such behavior is not a form of self-preservation. It's just the opposite! It is only by connecting to our inner life and to the inner lives of others that we can live and love fully. Now is all we have. None of us knows what the future holds, but I do know that few of the calamities we dread ever happen. We can never see when or how the cruel hand of fate will strike. But when it does, it's sure to pitch a curveball that we never see coming. So why limp through life guarding against disasters that may never appear? We must stop straightjacketing our hearts and bracing for demons that never materialize. We must live life fully in the now, live like we're dying at each moment, and *love* like each day is our last—for love is the only currency of connection to this world and the beyond.

As I close this book, I know that the messages of love that Jean and I have written together will continue forever, as will our ministry. As Jean told me soon after leaving his body, *Now do you understand why you're Dr. Love? Because I can touch and love all the millions that you touch and love.* I pray that this book has served you well, and I welcome the opportunity to continue to assist you as you travel down the path to peace, love, and reconnection.

Appendix

My Patients' Dialogues with Spirit

Be bold
And allow your own dialogues to unfold

Tina and Gerry

A couple named Tina and Gerry came to see me for marriage counseling. They told me that he becomes frantic and worried when problems arise in their business. When he comes to her for comfort (something he never received as a child), what he receives instead is a litany of practical suggestions for how to solve the problem. When Tina responds that way, he becomes angry and turns away from her. She in turn becomes angry at his behavior. She added that a lifelong belief of hers is that something good can't last and ultimately will be taken away from her.

When she said that, I received a message that she was dealing with the loss of a loved one. "Who died?" I asked her.

She burst into tears and said, "My dad, when I was 12."

I told her that her grief had created a false belief system that nothing good can last because her daddy didn't last. He was taken away from her.

She cried again, and this time I went over to her and squeezed her shoulder. "Tina," I said softly, "your father hasn't left you. He's right here. He's been standing outside your door for all these years, waiting for you to let him in."

"How is that possible?" she choked, and so I told her the short version of Jean's and my story.

She shook her head in frustration. "I don't know how to do it."

"Yes, you do," I reassured her. "Be still and listen. It's like meditating."

At that moment, I heard her father's voice saying hello to her. She froze in disbelief. "I heard him," she gasped. "I heard him say hello to me."

Tina returned the next week with her husband and told me that her life had changed. She no longer felt hollow and empty. She said that she felt as though the circuits in her brain had been rewired. My taking the risk of telling her my story had made it possible for her to take the leap of faith.

On the ride home, she had asked her father why he died so young and left her mother widowed. Her father had answered, *That's her story, Tina.* She said that the words she heard felt like they were coming from outside her body, just as I had described what happens when Jean speaks to me.

She told me that she'd driven by her childhood home, bereft because her mother was selling it. She then heard her father say, *It's just a house.* The communication continued throughout the entire ride, but not after that. Tina was crestfallen because she hadn't felt or heard him since. He was gone.

"No, he's not," I assured her. "He's still here." Just then my electrical backup system began making a beeping sound—the sound it makes when there's a power failure, which there wasn't.

Tina and her husband both asked me what that sound was.

"It's your father's spirit," I said to Tina. "He's using electronic equipment to tell you he's here."

After a few minutes of listening to the racket, I stood up and walked over to the machine. "If I acknowledge your presence now," I said calmly, "I know that you will stop making this noise." Instantly the machine went silent. Gerry and Tina stared at each other slack jawed.

While I was delighted for Tina, the next morning I chided Jean for never making the machine beep for me. I had hardly finished my gentle tirade when the machine began beeping!

When I saw Tina the next week, she told me that she no longer sensed her father's presence. But there he was, sitting in a chair with his arms folded across his chest. I asked her if this was a normal posture for him when seated, and she said it was.

The following week, she described her mother as an "energy vampire" who always lived off her daughter and gained her excitement in life through her. Tina told her mother about contacting her dad, and rather than sharing in Tina's joy, her mother just wanted to hear all the details so that she could ride on her daughter's experience, rather than work on establishing her own connection.

Tina said that because of this, she stopped making contact with him. Talk about cutting off one's nose to spite one's face.

I counseled her, "Make contact, just don't tell your mother."

Tina was late for our next session. We talked about her pattern of cheating herself of the things she loves (such as yoga and her couples therapy). This sure seemed like self-punishment resulting from buried rage. Was she angry with her mother for having been such a burden? Because of her mother's weakness and Tina's feeling that she had to take care of her mother after her father died, she never rebelled as a teen. She protected her mother from her anger by keeping it locked inside herself. She punished herself for this buried rage with various acts of self-denial.

The following week, Tina came back feeling like a wreck. She said she felt as though she were having a nervous breakdown. She admitted that ever since her dad died when she was a child, she'd assumed the role of father without even knowing it. Her mother continued to play the helpless victim, along with her sister. Tina still felt pressure to take care of them both, since they both constantly asked her for financial help.

I clearly sensed that the pressure cooker of her anger at having to be the "savior" of her family was shattering her psyche. Because she was everyone else's caretaker, she'd never been able to express her own anger. It just got locked away inside herself.

I told her that she had to find a way to release her anger. Then I heard her father say, *I want her to back off,* meaning that he wanted her to stop playing multiple roles and connect with her true self. Next I heard him scolding her, calling her by her first name followed by another name, Dorothy, which I assumed was her middle name. I asked her if her father sometimes called her "Dorothy," and she said yes.

I asked her why.

"Because that's my middle name," she said.

Her father giving me her middle name was clearly his way of showing that he was still present, thereby proving that she didn't need to usurp his role. This she seemed to understand. It was a breakthrough—one of those supreme "now I get it" moments.

Several weeks later, Tina told me that she'd dreamed that a female friend of hers was smiling at her while sitting in her living room. The woman brought her father to her, and for the first time since he died, she really felt his presence. As he offered his hand to her, she felt a strong sense of peace and acceptance settle over her . . . and she still felt it when she awoke. This experience instantly enabled her to set boundaries and eliminated her sense of depletion in all her relationships.

Bernadette and Her Daughters

On my first visit to France after Jean left his body, I visited my old friend Bernard's widow, Bernadette, and her two daughters. The family was in chaos and had been since Bernard's death. The daughters couldn't speak about their pain in front of their mother because each time they tried to do so, she cut them off by claiming that her suffering was worse than theirs. Three years later,

Bernadette was still in a constant state of mourning, living alone in the house, never socializing, often telling her daughters that she no longer wanted to live.

Before arriving in France, I'd received a message from Bernard that he wanted me to give a piece of jewelry to each of "his girls." I told them this as I handed out the gifts. Fleur, the younger daughter, burst into tears.

I asked, "Have you been in touch with your father?" She said the mere mention of his name made her weep.

"This is because you haven't grieved his bodily loss. The feelings are still very fresh," I explained. I then assured her that her father wanted to reconnect to her.

Her mother overheard what I said and was completely opposed to the idea. I replied that her own grief would never cease until she reconnected to her husband.

She told me that she was raised a traditional Catholic and was taught to believe that she would have to wait until death to reunite with her husband in heaven. She added that she was afraid of what might happen if she went against the teachings of the church.

I then told her and her two daughters the story of Jean and me. As I went along, I could sense from their rapt attention that I was having a profound effect on all three. At the end, Bernadette jumped up and took my hand. She led me to the kitchen, where she showed me the overhead light above her stovetop. She said the light had broken, and when she instinctively asked her deceased husband to fix it, suddenly it worked perfectly. Interestingly, it came naturally to her to make the request despite her Catholic teachings.

She then took me from room to room like an excited child, recounting various signs of Bernard's presence that she had failed to recognize. She wept with joy when she told me that she realized that he was still with her. She said that henceforth she would begin talking to him and connecting with him.

Fleur wrote to me afterward to say that before my visit, they had all been feeling depressed and hopeless. Now all three feel light and happy. She said that she was talking to her daddy and that he had come to her in her dreams, which were both peaceful and meaningful, with no trace of sadness.

Elaine

Elaine came to visit me because she felt dead inside. She told me that she wanted to live life more fully instead of sleepwalking through each day. It soon became apparent to me what Elaine's problem was. She was anesthetizing herself against the rage she still felt toward her deceased mother, whom she described as a fragile, miserable, depressed woman who was more like a child than a parent. Elaine had to take care of her mother in a most depressing way. When her mom was alive, Elaine had been afraid to have a good time or laugh because if she did, her mother would be jealous of her. To protect her mother and to keep her on an even keel, Elaine had to hide her own needs and feelings.

Her mother also foisted her own negative feelings onto her daughter by picking fights with her at every opportunity and verbally ripping her to shreds. After each argument, her mother would collapse in a heap of guilty tears and beg for Elaine's forgiveness. Pity her as she might, Elaine was usually too angry to accept her mom's apology, let alone return her embrace. Eventually, all this pent-up emotion took its toll, and Elaine became bulimic.

I tried to help Elaine express her anger, but her pity for her mother prevented it. I then tried to help her develop a new relationship by dialoguing with her mother, but she was unwilling to do this, either because she wished to protect her or because she feared being abused again, just as she had been in years past. The best compromise we could achieve was for me to symbolically "take charge" of her mother for a period, in order to give Elaine a vacation from all the internal tyranny and turmoil.

One day I made a mistake. I forgot we had a session scheduled for that day. Elaine was angry with me but quickly turned her rage back on herself by saying that she was, among other things, unlovable.

Finally I asked, "Why do you assume my mistake has anything to do with you? Why don't you ask yourself what's wrong with Jamie?" I kept going: "Why don't you ask the same thing about your mother? What was wrong with her?"

This led Elaine to realize that her mother's behavior may have had nothing to do with Elaine being bad or unlovable. The abuse may have instead been the result of a physical or mental sickness.

A week later, Elaine came down with a cold. While sick abed, she told me that she heard her mother telling her she was a burden and useless.

I told Elaine that I certainly didn't feel that way, but my words were like water rolling off a duck's back. All she heard was her mom, and the internal voice of her mother now was identical to that of the mother of her childhood. She was stuck with the abusive mother in her head, and so she continued to be reinjured.

Based on this reality, it was clear that the only way for Elaine to heal was for her to develop a more evolved relationship with her mother. If she could feel loved and accepted by her mom, the wounded little girl could replace the old critical voice with a new loving and accepting one.

One day I said, "You know your mother never meant you harm. Now in spirit form, she is more knowing, seeing, and loving. I know she wants to be a better mother to you. She just needs your help and guidance." I asked her if she would be willing to let me help her mother work this out with her, and she agreed.

The next week we dialogued with her mother for the first time. At the start of the session, Elaine said she needed me to tell her mother something.

"Why won't you tell her yourself?" I urged.

She said that in the past her mother would often collapse when faced with confrontation. Elaine said that she wanted her mother to know that she is angry with her for taking her life from her.

Suddenly her mother came to her as a vision, and she saw in her mind's eye that her mother wasn't crying and wringing her hands, as she was wont to do when she was alive. This gave Elaine the courage to say, "I need you to tell me that you want me to enjoy my life. I need your blessing."

What happened then I will never forget. Elaine's face became fraught with emotion.

"What do you see?" I asked her softly.

"I see my mother," she whispered. "She is opening her arms to me and nodding."

Since that day, Elaine's mother has come often to her as a vision. She often sees the image of a sewing machine, which is a sign of her mother's presence. "Mom was always sewing," Elaine told me. She sees the machine also as a symbol of her mother supporting her efforts to be creative and joyful.

At the end of our work together, Elaine told me, "Birth and death are bookends on the shelf of my life. Realizing that I have read more books than I have books left to read [meaning that she was aware of her mortality and the fact that she was closer to the end of her life than the beginning of it], I am more able to live in the present and feel joy." She added, "I have begun to reread some of the books I have already read. But now when I reread them, I have a different perspective of the chapters of my life. I perceive my mother's actions very differently."

Elaine was at peace.

Chuck

Chuck, a man who didn't believe in God or the afterlife, lived his life depressed, anxious, and buried under a mountain of defeat, doom, and self-loathing. He was utterly alone and certain that he would never find a loving partner. He was married to his suffering and to his supposed fate.

In one group-therapy session, he told the story of his childhood idol, the Amazing Randy, a magician whom he'd adored. His father, now deceased, arranged to have the magician come to their house. Chuck was so excited to meet his idol, but just before Randy arrived, he was sent to bed. This, he informed the group, was the story of his life. He could never experience joy. He had to live each day according to the dictates of his father. Dad's word was the law. He always had the last say. He was the star, and everyone revered him. The father was smarter than Chuck, more handsome, and more successful in every aspect of life, including with women. Chuck never questioned his father's rule. He just paid homage to the king and allowed him to shine. Failure and suffering composed Chuck's ultimate sacrifice.

At a recent session, I told Chuck that he was a professional victim, meaning that he had learned to express his anger toward his father by turning it against himself. Each time he suffered, was depressed or anxious, or felt doomed with no hope of ever having a decent life, he was secretly telling his father, "You bastard, look at how you ruined my life."

As I told Chuck this, he listened attentively. Within minutes his expression brightened, and he said he'd never felt so free and lighthearted.

I explained that the only cure for him was to stop being the sacrificial lamb. He had to stop swallowing his anger against his father, stop turning rage back on himself, and instead own up to his fury toward his father for having screwed up his life.

I asked Chuck to explore why he was so willing to continue to be his father's slave rather than to stand up to him. Did he sacrifice himself because he sensed that even in death, his father's weak ego needed to be built up by putting his son down? No, Chuck said; his father was the king in his family and was simply used to being adulated.

Here's where the breakthrough occurred. I suddenly realized the hypocrisy of the situation. I looked him squarely in the eye and said, "You are worshipping a dead god. And you don't even believe in God!"

Upon Chuck hearing that remark, his eyes bulged. It was as though he finally understood the absurdity and futility of the sacrifices he continued to make. He began laughing when he told me that he actually saw hope for himself for the first time in his life.

Chuck's elation, however, deflated a few minutes later. He said that his father's voice came back to tell him that he was being ridiculous for thinking he could be free.

I urged Chuck to talk to his father, but he was afraid to. "My father always won every argument," he said dejectedly. "He turned around everything I said and told me I was wrong. I can't talk to him."

I reminded Chuck that since he doesn't believe that spirit lives on, he has no reason to fear an entity who no longer exists.

I summoned the adult Chuck to defend the little boy. I reminded Chuck that he isn't tiny anymore. The adult Chuck can speak on behalf of the child inside him who has never stood up to, or separated from, his father. It was time to talk to his dad and "de-deify" him.

With that Chuck went to town. He told his father, "The king is dead." I suggested he use humor to put his father in his place. For example, he might say, "I gave already . . ." I also said his new commandment should be "You shall have no other gods before me." As they laughed along, other members of the group offered their own contributions.

As Chuck continued standing up to his father, speaking aloud, defying his dad's rule, and asserting his new personality, the old Chuck faded away. He said good-bye to a lifetime of emotional slavery. He sat taller, and the ashen shade of his skin transformed into a youthful glow.

Chuck was reborn before our very eyes after dialoguing with his father.

Didi

Didi's dad died when she was 16. From his death until she came to see me at the age of 40, she lived in her own quasi-fantasyland. She behaved as though she were still a teenager. She was afraid to get married and have kids, as adults do. She lived in a state of denial in which she attempted to remain frozen in her youth, at the time before her daddy died. She knew that her father had gone, but her defense mechanisms kept her from fully facing it; therefore she never grieved for him.

To complicate matters, she was terrified of allowing herself to fully love her fiancé, Tim. She admitted that she'd loved her first boyfriend and he left her. So in her mind, if she admitted to Tim that she loved him, he'd leave her, too. She kept Tim at arm's length because she couldn't bear another loss. As a result, he began to withdraw from her and told her that he no longer wanted to marry. That's when she came to see me.

One of the first things she told me was how proud her father was of her and how confident he always made her feel. She said that since his death, her confidence had gone out the window. She wanted to love and be loved, but she lacked the self-assurance. I told her that she would never be able to feel confident until she reconnected to her father and let him back into her life.

Didi said she wanted to connect to him, but couldn't. I asked her why, even though I already knew what her answer would be: "Because if I do that, I am admitting he's dead."

"You have been living alone in an emotional desert," I told her, "unable to connect to your father or to Tim. If you're willing to admit that Dad is dead, grieve for him, and accept that his body is gone, then you can begin the process of reconnecting to him in spirit form. When you reconnect to him, the pride he has for you will shine through to you. You'll feel better about yourself, and you will finally be able to love."

She said she didn't know how to let her dad in, so I asked her to lie down on the couch, and I guided her into a meditative state. I had her imagine that she was lying on a beach. I told her that the sun was shining on her. I asked her to feel the heat pouring into her—the rays of the sun pouring her father's love into her, filling her with love, light, and confidence.

"Now breathe deeply. Feel his spirit entering your pores, your DNA.

His spirit is inside you. His love for you and confidence in you is now yours."

Didi entered a trance. Tears poured down her face. She told her father that she missed him. He said, through me, *I'm right here, Didi. It's time to be brave and accept that I'm gone in body, but here with you in spirit always.*

She said she saw a wispy shadow trimmed with green. Then she felt as though she were floating outside her body; lights were moving all around her.

I explained that she was in the spirit realm with him. That's how it feels to be outside one's body. Didi no longer needed to fear death. It's a wonderful and peaceful place.

Anytime you want to connect with me, he assured her, *just breathe deeply and you will find me.*

Hearing his words brought peace and love cascading through her.

I said on behalf of her father, *You can have this experience whenever you want it. You must promise me that you will come to me each day. You always kept your word to your father. Promise me now.*

And she did.

When Didi returned to her body, she felt reborn, light, and peaceful. The relationship with her fiancé began moving forward. She started wearing her engagement ring again, and she and Tim began looking for a house. She later had a child, and they are living happily ever after.

Sam

Sam's dad had a collapsed lung. As a child, Sam knew that his father developed palpitations and couldn't breathe if he became upset. Whenever Sam misbehaved, his mother said to him, "Now look what you've done to your father!"

Sam learned to walk on eggshells and button his lip to not upset his dad. He truly believed that strong emotions would kill his father. Seven decades later with his father long gone, Sam still lived in an emotional straightjacket, repressing his feelings—especially his anger. He came to therapy because he couldn't live like this any longer. Individual and group therapy sessions had gone a long way toward helping him. Although he was able to express his feelings to me and other group members, I sensed that for him to be truly free, he needed to dialogue with his father.

I told him that the spirit lives on and that his dad was waiting to connect with him. There was no longer any risk, I reminded him: "You can't kill your father since he's already dead!" Sam still remained reticent, scared to express himself to his father.

"Before I can talk to Dad," he said, "I need to take off the protective armor I've been wearing my entire life."

So we put the dialoguing on hold.

Several months later, Sam told me he was miserable. His wife scorned him for being detached and aloof, but instead of fighting back, he withdrew entirely from her, which triggered more angry accusations.

I asked him to imagine going into his father's room and talking to him.

Sam had never spoken his heart to his father. He suddenly felt chills, and I saw gooseflesh on his arms. His father's spirit was there with us.

I told Sam that he could talk to his father now in a way that was not possible when the man was alive.

Hesitantly, Sam told his father that he was sorry his dad was ill, but that he was a kid and needed to live his life. Kids make mistakes, and he shouldn't have been made to feel responsible for what happened to his father. As he said this, Sam broke down in tears. He told me that somehow life had been breathed into his lungs, which had been constricted since childhood.

Later that session, Sam described a dream from the night before in which he opened a large steel door and found his dead mother on the other side.

I suddenly felt a chill and realized that his mother had visited him in order to help him further his healing. I felt her presence and saw her face.

I said, "Your mother knows that you're angry with her for teaching you to stifle your emotions, and she wants you to talk to her about it."

"I know she did the best she could," he said, "and although I feel guilty about it, I just can't speak to her."

Sam recounted that one day when he was young, he dawdled while playing with a friend and came home later than he was supposed to. When he arrived home, his mother was waiting at the door. She chewed him out and laid a guilt trip on him. She said, "Your father was so upset and now he can't breathe."

I asked Sam to tell his mother now what he would have liked to say then. Suddenly the floodgates opened, and his rage toward her poured out. Afterward, he wept in relief.

I then heard his mother say in Yiddish, *Zei gezunt.* I asked Sam if his mother used to say those words.

"Yes, she did," he said. "It means 'go forth in health.'" This was his mother's way of telling him how happy she was that he'd finally broken the vow of silence that had been destroying his emotional health.

Sam's dialoguing with his dead father and mother was the source of his healing. He felt alive and his marriage improved. Since he was present to himself and his feelings, his wife no longer needed to belittle him for his lifelong pattern of passivity and distancing.

Mo

One Thanksgiving, I talked to an Asian woman named Mo who had lost her husband in September 2001. She was still missing him years later, especially on this, their anniversary week.

I told her Jean's and my story, and she replied by stating flat out that her husband wasn't present.

"Yes, he is, Mo," I insisted. "He *is* present, and he always has been. He's just waiting for you to open your door to him."

I sensed she wasn't aware of the signs of spirit presence. I enumerated some of the signs—gooseflesh, temperature changes, thoughts popping in her head, and animal messengers. I then instructed her in how to create the right climate to connect with him.

She wept and thanked me profusely. Simply telling her our story, teaching her how to create the right atmosphere for connection, and familiarizing her with the signs changed her outlook.

I saw Mo again at Thanksgiving the following year. I asked her if she had been in contact with her husband. She said that she'd been too busy to make time.

"We always have so much to do," I sympathized. "We just have to make the time for something so important."

I then heard her husband say, *She won't do it for herself, but she'll do it for me.*

I told Mo that her husband wanted her to be a better wife to him and that he would not rest until she connected with him.

She agreed that while it wouldn't be easy for her, she would do it for him.

When I heard him say that he wanted her to marry again, and told Mo this, I sensed her resistance. She said that in her culture it is considered disloyal to remarry. I told her that her husband said he didn't agree. She felt confused.

"If I remarry," she asked, "whom will I reunite with in heaven?"

I explained to her that envy and jealousy don't exist in heaven. There's no limit to the number of people we can love. Heavenly love is infinite, not possessive. In spirit, earthly laws do not bind us.

I then asked if she wanted me to show her how to dialogue with her husband.

She said yes, so I helped her enter a trance. I asked her to close her eyes and breathe deeply. I guided her to allow the breath to move through her body. Starting from the top of her head, I had her visualize the breath bathing her in a warm, golden light. "Imagine the breath warming your muscles, melting them like taffy in the sun," I soothed. "With each exhalation, see the tension draining from your body and being expelled from your fingertips and toes." I told her to let me know when she felt fully relaxed.

Finally she opened her eyes and said, "I can't seem to connect to him."

"Yes you can," I said. "Let go and trust yourself. Open your heart, breathe, and feel him. It's okay."

At that moment, I heard her husband say, "I'm holding your hand."

Suddenly, her left hand reached out. "I feel him," she gasped. "I really *feel* him."

"I know," I said. "He's touching your heart."

She said, "I feel that, too."

Her face flushed and looked filled with light. Then her mood shifted, and she appeared crestfallen. She said she'd experienced a "heavy feeling."

"You are grieving," I explained, "and grieving is a lonely activity. You must not be alone with the grief. You must share it with your husband. You can connect with him in spirit form and still grieve with him the loss of his earthly body." I paused and then said, "There seems to be a block to you staying connected with him. Do you know why that is?"

"It's because he's in heaven. I never felt it was possible." She told me that her culture taught that "heaven is a palace in the clouds," meaning that it is beyond human reach.

I told her that the image of a palace in the clouds is a human fabrication, an attempt to represent the afterlife using earthly images. I repeated for her benefit the words that Jean had often said to me: "Heaven is a state, not a place. Death is an illusion; there is a very thin veil between the realm where you are and the realm where I am."

She told me that her husband had explained to her while he was alive that heaven is a parallel universe. But what I had described intuitively made more sense to her.

"I think I can connect to him now," she said, and after that day she did indeed connect with him, in most meaningful ways.

Dawn

While conducting a group-therapy session toward the end of 2013, I noticed that one of my patients, Dawn, who is a nurse, was highly distressed. I asked her what was wrong.

She replied that in the past week her best friend, Elsie, who was like a sister to her, had died without warning. She went on to explain that she and Elsie and a group of mutual female friends had just gone for their annual ladies' day at Foxwoods Casino in Connecticut. On the way back home, Elsie, who was driving her own car, said that one of her tires was having trouble and she needed to stop to put air in it.

Dawn and another member of their party pulled into the service station behind Elsie. After filling her tire, Elsie announced that she wanted to go to Walmart to purchase a temporary patch kit. Assured that someone was going to drive behind Elsie and stay with her until her chore was finished, Dawn said good-bye to her best friend and headed home.

Not long afterward, my patient received a frantic call from the woman who had accompanied Elsie to Walmart.

"You have to hurry back," the woman said. "Something is terribly wrong with Elsie. She collapsed on the ground and is having a seizure."

As Dawn raced back to the store, the other woman, who's also a nurse, performed CPR on Elsie. But by the time my patient arrived at the scene, Elsie was dead.

Dawn wept as she described seeing her friend on the pavement, her eyes rolled back in her head and her clothing soiled with urine. Ever since the tragedy, Dawn and the other woman had been berating themselves nonstop for failing to save Elsie.

At the moment Dawn shared her feelings of guilt with the group, Elsie came through like gangbusters. Clearly, she was hellbent (or should I say heaven sent?) on talking with my patient and setting her straight.

First, Elsie described in nontechnical terms what had happened to her. Knowing that Dawn and her other friend are both nurses, it would have been logical to assume that Elsie was a nurse, too. So I was confused when I began to hear Elsie's description of her condition.

"She doesn't sound like she's a nurse," I said. "She's struggling to explain what happened to her."

Dawn confirmed that Elsie hadn't been a nurse.

Elsie then told me that her friends were wrong to blame themselves. She said that she'd had bleeding in her brain and was dead before she hit the ground. The CPR was artificially keeping her alive. She reassured Dawn that she suffered no pain.

Next, she showed me the image of the tire on her car. She said that what happened in her brain was the same thing that happened to the inner tube of her tire—it bulged and blew. Dawn then confirmed that Elsie's symptoms were consistent with a brain aneurism, which was exactly what her friend was describing.

Elsie went on to say that Dawn shouldn't be sad. I heard her use the expression "chin up." She kept repeating this—she clearly wanted my patient to snap out of her reverie of agony and guilt. *There was nothing that anyone could have done,* she said.

"She was *always* telling me to keep my chin up. Those were her words!" Dawn exclaimed.

Suddenly, Elsie showed me that she was kicking up her heels, first to the left and then to the right. Dawn explained that this image must be her way of communicating the fact she was finally free to move and dance about. In Elsie's earthly body, she had suffered many broken bones and was essentially crippled.

Elsie went on to say that she made the choice to leave her body in that way. If she hadn't done so, she would have suffered a terribly painful death.

When Dawn heard this, she said, "Oh my gosh. The week before, she asked me if I would take care of her dog and plants if she died! What she's saying now confirms that she indeed chose to pass on."

At this point, Elsie showed me the image of a four-leaf clover, so I asked Dawn if Elsie was Irish.

"No," she said. "Elsie was Jewish and Portuguese!"

I thought, *I must be losing it! Where did I get the Irish connection from?*

But just then Dawn added that Elsie often wore an Irish four-leaf clover that Dawn had given her as a gift. It was a prized possession, so Elsie offered the image to confirm her presence and reassure Dawn. By this point, I was crying along with the rest of the group.

My tears were soon stopped by the next image—which was of big boobs. For the life of me, I could not figure out why this picture was being implanted in my mind.

I sheepishly asked, "Did Elsie have big breasts?"

Despite her mix of raw emotions, Dawn emitted a sharp laugh. "She sure did! They were enormous!"

I realized that Elsie was showing me this distinguishing feature in order to further prove her presence. She also showed them to me in order to give the message that she was a maternal figure to Dawn—the mother that she never had—again to further validate her presence.

When I said this, Dawn confirmed, "That's the truth!"

The next thing Elsie said was, *You better save a place for me at Thanksgiving.* Then she planted the oddest image in my mind: a turkey drumstick.

I asked, "Is she obsessed with drumsticks? I hear her insisting that you save her the drumstick."

We all gasped when Dawn confirmed that they went to the diner every week, and Elsie always ordered a drumstick!

By offering such explicit details, Elsie wanted to reassure Dawn that she was right there. I explained that she was just in a different form in much the same way that water converts to ice or steam.

Then I heard a bizarre vibration emanating from my waiting room. I opened the door, and an antique metal eyeglass box was visibly vibrating. This had happened once before when the spirit of another group patient came through.

All six group members stood with me and watched in astonishment as the eyeglass container continued to shake and vibrate. There was no earthly reason to explain what was causing this to happen. I have no washer or dryer or anything else mechanical in the room or adjacent rooms. The only possible explanation was that Elsie was confirming my statement that she had converted into her new energetic form.

A couple of days later, I received an e-mail from Dawn thanking me profusely for the experience we shared in group.

"I have finally achieved peace with what happened to Elsie," she wrote. "I feel as though a great weight has been taken off of my shoulders and I am feeling like myself again."

EULOGY

Following is a eulogy I gave in memory of my husband, Jean Pin, on September 23, 2006. May it serve as a bookend to this work, along with the dedication page at the beginning.

My beloved Jean, I'll never forget the day I met you. I was a young freshman at Vassar College. I really wanted to take Intro Soc—but all the sections were full. You were the department chair and your secretary told me to go to your office and ask if an exception could be made. I never believed in love at first sight . . . until I walked into your office. You were the most beautiful man I'd ever seen, not just physically. You radiated such inner beauty, kindness, and gentleness. You immediately added a seat in *your* class.

During lectures I was amazed at how this meek man magically transformed into a mesmerizing lecturer who held us all in rapt attention at the edge of our seats. Suddenly in the midst of your oration, you would stop dead in your tracks and look to me to see if what you had said made sense. You were so humble; you, this brilliant, highly educated professor, were looking to *me*, a lowly freshman. One day you stopped the lecture and said, "Jamie is furrowing her brow, which means I wasn't clear. Let me try saying it another way." You always honored me and made me feel like the most brilliant woman on earth. Four years later, I needed help with the statistical portion of my senior thesis and my advisor didn't know statistics. I asked if you could help, and even though I wasn't your advisee, you cheerfully gave me your time. In the weeks that passed, we fell madly in love.

Despite our different cultures, religions, and the vast age difference, we were completely compatible. Twins separated at birth. Soul mates. We loved the same activities, music, books, and hobbies. We wrote books *together*, ran businesses *together*, restored and decorated houses *together*, and rejoiced in every moment that we spent *together*. We were inseparable. You have been by my side, my loyal and beloved supporter at every moment of our life. Whenever I was down, you wrapped me in your arms and really listened to me with such patience, gentleness, and acceptance. I asked you recently, "How can you give me so much?," and you said, "I just love you, Jamie." If you ever said or did something to upset me, you'd tell me, "I promise for as long as I live to work on changing that aspect of myself." And you did keep your word. Every day of your life was a quest for perfection; you were like an innocent child, an open book, seeking to know more, to learn more, to grow more, all with the intention of being a better and more loving husband (as if that were possible).

In August when I was doing a juice fast and needed a special organic ingredient found only in a faraway health-food store, you drove an hour each way after a long day of work to get the item for me. When I thanked you, you said, "I love to be able to help you."

Your capacity for love wasn't of this earth. You are an endless well of giving. For all of our 27 years together, even up until last week, you'd call me each Wednesday morning and say, "Is Jamie there?" And I'd say, "Yes." And you'd say, "Are you free for a date? I hope that I called you early enough and that another guy hasn't asked you out already."

When I returned from Italy alone, without you, I was so broken. Then I opened the folder that you had labeled In Case, and read your last line, which said, "I'm not here anymore, but wherever I am I'll always watch over you and love you immensely."

My dear Jean, I will always love you. You are my north, my south, my east, and my west.

ACKNOWLEDGMENTS

I want to express my sincerest thanks to Laurie Harper. Despite coming on board very recently, you made me feel as though we'd worked together for decades. You instantly understood the importance of this book and magically opened all the right doors. Working with you, Laurie, has been one of the most enjoyable and effortless literary experiences I've ever encountered. You are so gifted at what you do. I wish you every happiness and success.

I am also grateful to Brent Robison, a gifted writer in his own right, who is very conversant with the latest scientific research into energetic communications. He kindly read my chapter on this topic and provided me with links to the top scientists who are studying the topic of soul survival.

I also wish to express my deep gratitude to my brilliant editor, William C. Hammond. No matter what I throw at you, you have the chameleon-like ability to adjust your writing style so that your edits are indistinguishable from my own voice. Your loving dedication to my ministry and message has been a blessing for which I give daily thanks.

Thanks also to my new "Stiletto Sisters," who recently entered my life. You have brought me so much love, joy, and support of our new ministry.

Last but not least, I want to thank Stacey Smith, Diane Ray, Melissa Brinkerhoff, Erin Dupree, Celeste Phillips, Johanne Mahaffey, Shay Lawry, Elizabeth Kelley, Christy Salinas, Heather Tate, Shannon Godwin, Shannon Littrell, Bea Camarena, Richelle Zizian, and the entire Hay House staff for helping me birth this baby. I am especially grateful to my editor, Alex Freemon. Given how close I am to the material in this book, you offered excellent suggestions on how to organize the book so as to make my information most accessible to my readers.

Of course, I give thanks to all my beloved patients who have opened their hearts to me and granted me the permission to disclose their stories, which, I hope, will further assist my dear readers to step through the gates of heaven so that they, too, may experience their own healing miracles.

Many thanks also to my friend Roberta Grimes, renowned afterlife researcher and author, who kindly read my expanded discussion of the science of survival of consciousness and suggested a few editorial modifications.

About the Author

Known to millions as Dr. Love, through her immensely popular website, AskDrLove.com—the web's first relationship-advice site, online since 1995—**Jamie Turndorf, Ph.D.,** has been delighting readers and audiences for three decades with her engaging blend of professional knowledge, spicy humor, and ability to turn clinical psychobabble into easy-to-understand concepts that transform lives and heal relationships. She's recently brought this expertise to another level, pioneering a new grief-therapy method and assisting clients with after-death communications.

Jamie's conflict-resolution techniques have been featured on all the major networks, including CNN (who recently dubbed her their "Resident Love Doctor"), NBC, CBS, VH1, and Fox, and on WebMD, Discovery.com, and iVillage. She's also appeared in many of the most popular national magazines, such as *Cosmopolitan, Men's Health,* and *Glamour.* In addition, she writes a column called We Can Work It Out for *Psychology Today* online.

The *Ask Dr. Love* radio show can be heard in Seattle on KKNW and on Transformation Talk Radio, heard in 80 countries worldwide.

We hope you enjoyed this Hay House book. If you'd like to receive our online catalog featuring additional information on Hay House books and products, or if you'd like to find out more about the Hay Foundation, please contact:

Hay House, Inc., P.O. Box 5100, Carlsbad, CA 92018-5100
(760) 431-7695 or (800) 654-5126
(760) 431-6948 (fax) or (800) 650-5115 (fax)
www.hayhouse.com® • www.hayfoundation.org

———

Published in Australia by: Hay House Australia Pty. Ltd.,
18/36 Ralph St., Alexandria NSW 2015
Phone: 612-9669-4299 • *Fax:* 612-9669-4144
www.hayhouse.com.au

Published in the United Kingdom by: Hay House UK, Ltd.,
The Sixth Floor, Watson House, 54 Baker Street, London W1U 7BU
Phone: +44 (0)20 3927 7290 • *Fax:* +44 (0)20 3927 7291
www.hayhouse.co.uk

Published in India by: Hay House Publishers India,
Muskaan Complex, Plot No. 3, B-2, Vasant Kunj, New Delhi 110 070
Phone: 91-11-4176-1620 • *Fax:* 91-11-4176-1630
www.hayhouse.co.in

———

Access New Knowledge.
Anytime. Anywhere.

Learn and evolve at your own pace
with the world's leading experts.

www.hayhouseU.com

Free e-newsletters
from Hay House, the Ultimate
Resource for Inspiration

Be the first to know about Hay House's free downloads, special offers, giveaways, contests, and more!

 Get exclusive excerpts from our latest releases and videos from *Hay House Present Moments*.

 Our *Digital Products Newsletter* is the perfect way to stay up-to-date on our latest discounted eBooks, featured mobile apps, and Live Online and On Demand events.

 Learn with real benefits! *HayHouseU.com* is your source for the most innovative online courses from the world's leading personal growth experts. Be the first to know about new online courses and to receive exclusive discounts.

 Enjoy uplifting personal stories, how-to articles, and healing advice, along with videos and empowering quotes, within *Heal Your Life*.

Sign Up Now!

Get inspired, educate yourself, get a complimentary gift, and share the wisdom!

Visit www.hayhouse.com/newsletters to sign up today!

HAY HOUSE

HAY HOUSE
online learning

Printed in the United States
by Baker & Taylor Publisher Services